WHIMSICAL TREATS

FAIRY FOOD

TREATS FOR FANCIFUL MEALS & PARTIES

WHIMSICAL TREATS

FAIRY FOOD

Treats for Fanciful Meals & Parties

60 RECIPES FROM FLOWER FAIRIES, FOREST SPRITES & SEA NYMPHS

MARIE W. LAWRENCE

PHOTOS BY ABIGAIL GEHRING

Skyhorse Publishing

Skyhorse Publishing books may be purchased in bulk at special discounts for sales promotion, corporate gifts, fund-raising, or educational purposes. Special editions can also be created to specifications. For details, contact the Special Sales Department, Skyhorse Publishing, 307 West 36th Street, 11th Floor, New York, NY 10018 or info@skyhorsepublishing.com.

Skyhorse® and Skyhorse Publishing® are registered trademarks of Skyhorse Publishing, Inc.®, a Delaware corporation.

Visit our website at www.skyhorsepublishing.com.

10 9 8 7 6 5 4 3 2 1

Library of Congress Cataloging-in-Publication Data

Names: Lawrence, Marie W, author.

Title: Fairy food : treats for fanciful meals & parties / Marie W Lawrence.

Description: New York: Skyhorse Publishing, 2020. | Series: Whimsical treats | Includes index. | Summary: "Explore the whimsical world of fairy food in this delightful cookbook. Whether you're planning a fairy-themed party or just wish to add an element of fancy to your meals, you'll find plenty to inspire you here, from breakfasts and lunches to teatime to dessert"—Provided by publisher.

Identifiers: LCCN 2020000077 (print) | LCCN 2020000078 (ebook) | ISBN 9781510755949 (hardcover) | ISBN 9781510759367 (epub)

Subjects: LCSH: Cooking. | Entertainments.

Classification: LCC TX714 .L3923 2020 (print) | LCC TX714 (ebook) | DDC 641.5—dc23

LC record available at https://lccn.loc.gov/2020000077

LC ebook record available at https://lccn.loc.gov/2020000078

Cover design and photo by Abigail Gehring

Print ISBN: 978-1-5107-5594-9

Ebook ISBN: 978-1-5107-5936-7

Printed in China

For Anna and William. Always take time to play with the fairies!
With much love,
Granny

CONTENTS

INTRODUCTION

Fairies are fascinating little creatures who seem to have been around ever since humans can remember. There are numerous clans and subsets of fairies, and they are known by a variety of names. Many fairies co-exist happily with their human counterparts. Some are quite helpful and friendly, while others prefer a more private or solitary existence. Unfortunately, there have been a few instances over the centuries of fairies who didn't get along particularly well with people, or sometimes even with each other! I suppose, just as there are occasionally grumpy people, every once in a while there can also be grumpy fairies.

Many fairies have origins in northern Europe, where they can be found in forests, meadows, near or in the water, or even high on mountains. The European fairies, and also the fairy relatives in North America, frequently have developed specialized lifestyles, depending on the locations they inhabit. These may include, among others, garden fairies, orchard fairies, meadow fairies, woodland elves, and a number of unique water fairies such as sprites and nymphs.

Here in rural New England, fairy habitats abound. In recent years, it has become popular for many humans, both young and old, to construct fairy houses, in hopes of attracting some to live nearby. What fun to create, and for the fairies to discover!

One thing all fairies have in common is a love of delicious food. I have discovered that many of them are vegetarians, although some of the wilder forest fairies will harvest an occasional game bird for special feasts, and many of the water fairies enjoy reeling in fresh fish to add variety to their menus. Almost all fairies love dairy products such as milk, butter, and cheese, and eggs are another of the fairies' favorites. Nuts and mushrooms are other important fairy food sources.

They also love sweets! Fruits, berries, and wild honey are sure to keep almost any fairy happy for hours on end. A nibble of cake or pastry will make them positively joyous! I have included a number of fairy-friendly desserts for that very reason.

Many fairy foods also reflect other things that make fairies happy, such as flowers, rainbows, butterflies, and bubbles. Fairy fare is often on the light side; perhaps a bowl of hot soup in the winter, or cool salad during the summer months.

While most of the dishes in *Fairy Foods* are vegetarian, there are a few that utilize powdered gelatin. I don't believe the fairies will mind, especially since they have helped in the creation of so many recipes! Pixies, brownies, and water sprites have contributed several ideas, while the industrious farmland dairy fairies, garden fairies, berry fairies, and fruit fairies have made sure plenty of fresh ingredients were available for preparation purposes.

Some of the recipes included in *Fairy Foods* utilize pre-made ingredients such as refrigerated biscuit dough, making them quick and easy to prepare. Others give you the opportunity to make from-scratch special breads, cakes, cookies, and jams.

We hope you enjoy exploring *Fairy Foods*. The fairies and I wish you many happy adventures in cooking and creating!

FAIRIES' SUNRISE SELECTIONS

When the fairies first rise in the morning, they are always hungry for something delicious to start their day. Fun-loving and creative, they will frequently use a bit of fairy magic to turn ordinary breakfast foods into splendid little dishes that taste as amazing as they look. Because fairies are so very busy and industrious, they make a point of enjoying a hearty breakfast every morning. They understand that the best way for fairies, and people, to have a wonderful day, is to begin it with something wonderful to eat.

Pixie Pinwheels

MAKES 24 PINWHEELS.

Pixies are playful little folk who seem to live mostly in the south of England. Although some sources indicate they are a separate subgroup from the larger bands of fairies, I prefer to think of them as simply one of the many variations on the woodland clans. Surely any pixie would enjoy these edible pinwheels, which are grand fun for a special, fairy-themed breakfast. Although they are quite tasty, and pretty to look at, be forewarned that they simply will not spin in the wind! The filling makes enough for two dozen pinwheels. If you prefer to make up only eight at a time, extra filling can be refrigerated in a tightly covered container for up to a week. Filled, unbaked pinwheels may also be frozen for future use. Freeze them flat on a baking sheet, and if to be stored more than a few days, transfer to a covered, labeled container. Bake the frozen pinwheel pastries as below, adding a few minutes extra baking time.

3 (8-ounce) tubes refrigerated, unbaked
　　crescent rolls
8 ounces cream cheese
¼ cup granulated sugar
1 teaspoon vanilla extract
¼ teaspoon pure lemon or almond
　　flavoring, optional
1 large egg
1 teaspoon cornstarch
4½ cups confectioner's sugar, optional
½ cup + 1 tablespoon water, optional
24 pretzel rods
6 cups (total) pink strawberry &/or white
　　vanilla-flavored candy melts
Blueberries, small strawberries, raspberries,
　　sweet cherries, etc. for decorating
　　pinwheels

1. Keep the crescent roll dough refrigerated until just before you are ready to use it for best results. Preheat oven to 375°, adjusting the rack to an upper-middle position.

2. Place the cream cheese, sugar, and flavorings in a mixer bowl and beat until they are smooth and creamy. If you have a paddle attachment on the mixer, this works especially well. Add the egg and beat again, scraping down the sides of the bowl and beater a few times, as needed.

3. Slowly beat in the cornstarch until everything is nice and smooth. Set aside.

4. Gently unroll one tube of the crescent dough, but do not separate into triangles. (Placing it on an ungreased baking sheet will make the process of forming the dough go more smoothly, as you won't need to transfer the filled pinwheels.)

5. Press the perforations together to form a large rectangle; gently press and push to make a rectangle about twice as long as it is wide. A tiny bit of flour may help keep it from sticking to the baking sheet or cutting board, but could also make it harder for the premade perforations to adhere to each other.

6. Using a sharp knife, cut the dough into 8 smaller squares. Slice a line from the tip of each square's corner diagonally towards the center of the dough, leaving a small area in the center uncut. The cuts will leave you with four sections of dough that look almost like triangles (the tips would be in the center, where you didn't cut the dough).

7. Divide the filling into thirds (you'll use one third for each tube of dough). Take one third of the filling and mound it in the centers of the eight squares. To form each pinwheel, lift the left corner only of each "triangle," pinching it with the left corner next to it. Continue around the dough until all four corners have been pinched together, and then center the pinched ends gently on the cream cheese filling. You should now see the pinwheels you have just shaped from the dough! Repeat steps 1–7 with the other two tubes of dough.

8. Bake for about 15–20 minutes, until the pinwheels are golden brown and the filling is set. Remove from the oven and carefully, using a wide spatula, remove them to cooling racks.

9. Now you may finish your pinwheels however you wish. For plain glazed pinwheels, stir together the confectioner's sugar and water. Drizzle some decoratively over each pinwheel. Allow them to cool at least ten minutes; the filling will be hot, and the pinwheels very tender. Enjoy at room temperature or chilled; refrigerate any leftovers.

10. To make Pixie Pinwheel Wands: Make sure the pinwheels have had a chance to cool in advance. Microwave or gently heat the candy melts according to directions on the package. Stir until creamy.

11. Turn cooled pinwheels so that the back of each is up. Place about 1 tablespoon of the melted mixture on each pinwheel back. Dip each pretzel rod into the candy melts, spooning them up to cover ½ to ⅔ of each pretzel, and center one rod on the back of each pinwheel. Add a bit more of the melted mixture to anchor the pretzel well to the pinwheel. Reserve any leftover melts at room temperature while chilling the pinwheels to harden the bond.

12. Once you can pick the pinwheels up, turn them to again face front side up. Reheat the remaining candy melts and dab some on each in a pleasing pattern, positioning fresh berries on each spot of candy melt. (Use only whole berries; cut strawberries will become too juicy.) Chill again until they are ready to be enjoyed! These will last nicely in the refrigerator overnight, although for best results should be eaten within a day or two.

Blooming Honey Biscuits

MAKES 8 BISCUITS.

As we all know, fairies love honey. They will frequently befriend wild bees in hopes of sharing a bit of the sticky, sweet, golden liquid the bees so cleverly produce. Fairies are quite fond of seeds, too, gathering many varieties throughout the summer and fall. Here is a quick and easy way to combine two fairy favorites into one tasty breakfast treat!

2 tubes refrigerated, unbaked jumbo size
    butter flake biscuits (preferably honey
    flavor)
1 large egg
1 tablespoon milk
¼ cup hulled sunflower seeds
Honey for drizzling over top

1. Preheat the oven to 350°; place the oven racks in middle to upper positions.

2. Beat the egg with a fork until the yolk and white are well blended. Add the milk and stir it again to mix together. Pour the egg mixture into a pie pan or other shallow container that will give you room to dip the biscuits.

3. One at a time, dip each biscuit into the egg mixture to coat the top and sides, but not the bottom. Place half the egg-coated biscuits on two large, ungreased baking sheets, leaving lots of room in between each biscuit. Carefully sprinkle the sunflower seeds on top of these biscuits.

4. Place the remaining egg dipped biscuits on a cutting board and carefully, using a sharp knife, cut each biscuit in half, then into fourths and finally into eight pieces each. They will look like little triangles. Place the eight pieces from each cut biscuit around one of the biscuits on the baking sheets, pressing the egg dipped edges together slightly so that they look like little sunflowers.

5. Bake the biscuits for about 16–18 minutes, until they are golden brown and baked through. Carefully loosen them from the baking sheet while they are still hot, just in case some of the egg has leaked down and made them stick a bit. Remove them with a broad spatula, so that none of the petals loosen! Serve warm with honey drizzled over the top of each biscuit. Garnish with Fondant Honeybees (page 123), if you wish.

Egg-in-a-Hole

MAKES 1 SERVING.

Eggs are an important part of the fairies' diet. Although the fairies carefully harvest wild bird's eggs, people almost always use chicken eggs. It is actually illegal for humans to take most wild bird's eggs from their nests, because many years ago, people collected songbird eggs as a hobby. They didn't understand, as the fairies do, that most eggs need to be left in the nest. It was not good for the birds to lose so many of their eggs, so a law was passed protecting them. Egg-in-a-Hole is one of the fairies' favorite ways to enjoy a nice, fresh egg. Just remember to use a big slice of bread, so that you have room for the egg hole in the middle. A round cookie cutter, about 3 inches in diameter, works well for cutting out the hole. The top of a drinking glass can also be used, or you can cut a square hole with a sharp knife. A wide spatula will help you turn your bread and egg more easily.

1 tablespoon ketchup
1 tablespoon mayonnaise
Assorted cherry tomatoes and grape
 tomatoes
Fresh basil leaves
1 large slice bread
1 fresh egg
Butter
Salt & pepper

1. Mix together the ketchup and mayonnaise. Set aside.

2. Wash 3–4 grape or cherry tomatoes and slice each in half. Place them decoratively on one side of a dinner plate and arrange a couple of basil leaves around them to make a bouquet.

3. Use a heavy skillet or frying pan for frying your bread and egg; cast iron works really well. Warm the pan over medium heat. Melt about a teaspoon of butter, pushing it around so it resembles the shape of the bread slice you're using.

4. Place the bread on top of the melted butter and immediately cut out your egg hole, using the round cookie cutter. Place the cut-out bread, butter side down, next to the slice in the pan. Add a dab more butter into the hole in the bread.

5. Quickly break your egg into the hole and season it with a little salt and pepper. Break the yolk with the spatula, to help it cook evenly. (Some fairies and people used to like to keep the yolk runny to dip their bread into. Unfortunately, once in a while an uncooked egg may contain bacteria that could give folks who eat undercooked eggs a type of food poisoning called salmonella. That is why we recommend that you cook the yolk until it's firm.)

6. As the egg begins to set (the white of the egg will begin to turn white), add a little more butter to the pan. Flip over the bread round you cut from the center. Then, carefully, using the spatula, turn over the bread and egg. Cook a couple of minutes longer, until both sides of the bread are toasty and the egg is fried.

7. Place the fried egg and bread on the plate next to the tomato bouquet, place the fried center of the bread partially on the egg, and serve with your ketchup and mayonnaise sauce.

Jam-Filled French Toast Flowers

MAKES 1 SERVING.

Summer is such a glorious time for the fairies! Fresh eggs, milk, and cream are all in abundance, as are a wonderful variety of fresh berries and fruits. After the fairies have concocted a batch or two of Crimson Berry Jam, they frequently celebrate with a special summer breakfast featuring Jam-Filled French Toast Flowers. Of course, if you make enough jam, you can enjoy this pretty treat any time of the year!

2 large slices firm white bread
1 large egg
2 tablespoons milk or half-and-half
1 teaspoon sugar
¼ teaspoon pure vanilla extract
¼ teaspoon grated orange or lemon zest
   (or ⅛ teaspoon natural flavoring)
Sliced almonds, optional
Butter for frying
Crimson Berry Jam (page 79) or other
   favorite jam for filling
Confectioner's sugar for dusting over top

1. Cut each slice of bread with a large flower-shaped cookie cutter. The bread scraps can be saved and used for croutons, stuffing, or bread pudding.

2. In a shallow dish, beat the egg with a fork or whisk until the white and yolk are thoroughly combined. Stir in the milk, sugar, and flavorings until well combined but not foamy.

3. Heat a heavy skillet or frying pan over medium heat. Melt two small pats of butter in the pan. Dip the bread flowers into the egg mixture to absorb and coat completely. Place plain side down in the foaming butter.

4. Now press some sliced almonds into the top of each piece of French toast, if you wish. Melt a bit more butter and, when the French toast is lightly browned on one side, gently flip it over onto the buttered area. Continue frying in the butter until it is browned on both sides and cooked through.

5. Place one French toast flower, almond side down, on a serving plate. Spread it with a bit of the jam and gently place the other piece, almond side up, on top of it. Dust with a bit of confectioner's sugar and enjoy!

Rainbow-in-the-Clouds French Toast

MAKES 3 SERVINGS (OR POSSIBLY MORE FOR THOSE WITH FAIRY-LIKE APPETITES).

What could be better on a rainy day than to discover a rainbow peeking out from the clouds? It goes without saying that all fairies love rainbows. Sometimes a particularly adventuresome fairy may even try flying up to one, in hopes of sliding down the multi-colored bands of raindrops before they stop shimmering. That, of course, could only be accomplished by using a little fairy magic! If you'd like to bring a little fairy magic to your breakfast table, Rainbow-in-the-Clouds French Toast is a delicious way to accomplish that. A batch or two of Rainbow Tea Bread can easily be baked and sliced in advance, then popped in the freezer until it's time to enjoy this special treat. Hint: Rainbow-in-the-Clouds French Toast makes a lovely, light lunch or supper, too.

6 slices of Rainbow Tea Bread (page 43)
2 large eggs, lightly beaten
¼ teaspoon cinnamon
1 tablespoon honey or maple syrup
¼ cup milk or half-and-half
Oil for frying
Fresh blueberries
Spray whipped cream
Honey or maple syrup, optional

1. Beat the eggs and cinnamon with a whisk or fork until they are very well combined. Stir in the honey or maple syrup and the milk/cream, making sure the syrup or honey has blended in with the egg mixture.

2. Heat a small amount of oil in a heavy skillet or griddle over medium low heat. Dip each piece of bread into the egg mixture, coating both sides, placing as many as fit comfortably onto the hot skillet. Only dip what you'll be frying right away, as the bread will get soggy and may fall apart if left for too long.

3. Cook gently to set the egg custard, leaving one side lighter colored than the other (so that the rainbow colors still show through). Continue dipping and frying, adding oil as needed, until the French toast is all cooked.

4. Place two slices, colorful side up, on each of three plates. Place blueberry "raindrops" on top of the rainbows, and garnish with little clouds of whipped cream. This is already quite sweet, but can be served with additional honey or maple syrup, if you wish.

Garden Fairies' Rhubarb Porridge

MAKES 3 SERVINGS.

If you're the size of the average fairy, rhubarb can seem more like a tree than a plant in the garden. On hot summer days, more than one fairy has been known to relax in the shade of its luxuriant green leaves! When the rhubarb in the garden is still young and tender, garden fairies frequently gather enough of it to make this maple-sweetened breakfast treat. They combine the rhubarb with rolled oats, egg, milk, and flavorings, adding maple syrup to make it just sweet enough.

1¼ cups diced rhubarb
3 tablespoons butter, melted
1 large egg
⅞ cup milk
⅓ cup pure maple syrup
½ teaspoon vanilla extract
1 teaspoon grated orange zest
1 cup old-fashioned rolled oats
¼ teaspoon grated nutmeg
¼ teaspoon salt
½ teaspoon baking powder

1. Preheat oven to 350°. Dice the rhubarb and set it aside.

2. Melt the butter and use about 1 tablespoon of it to coat an 8-inch pie plate, casserole dish, or cake tin. Whisk the remaining butter with the egg, milk, maple syrup, vanilla, and orange zest.

3. In a small bowl, stir together the oats, nutmeg, salt, and baking powder; add to the liquid ingredients along with the diced rhubarb. Stir well and gently pour into the buttered baking pan.

4. Bake at 350° for about 40 minutes. The top will appear golden and the mixture will just be set. The edges may get a little crunchy, which is especially tasty! Serve warm or chilled. Refrigerate any leftovers.

WOODLAND FAIRIES' WILD BLUEBERRY MUFFINS

MAKES 12 REGULAR MUFFINS OR 36 MINI MUFFINS.

In the sun-dappled days of midsummer, woodland and garden fairies alike will frequently be found harvesting the scrumptious, fairy-sized fruits of wild blueberry bushes. Smaller and more intensely flavored than their domestic cousins, wild blueberries also have a slightly higher nutritional profile. Not to mention, they make wonderful wild blueberry muffins! The fairies add extra berries to their muffins, making them very blueberry indeed.

6 tablespoons butter

⅞ cup milk

1 teaspoon grated lemon zest or
    ½ teaspoon pure lemon extract

1 teaspoon pure vanilla extract

¼ teaspoon freshly grated nutmeg

2 eggs

2 cups all–purpose flour

¾ cup sugar

3 teaspoons baking powder

½ teaspoon salt

2 cups wild blueberries, fresh or frozen,
    thawed

1. Preheat oven to 375°, adjusting racks to upper-middle positions. Line 12 muffin cups or 36 mini muffin cups with correspondingly sized parchment cupcake wrappers. If using plain paper wrappers, it is helpful to spritz each one with a little non-stick cooking spray to prevent sticking. Alternative, the muffins cups can be well sprayed or buttered, rather than using the liners.

2. Melt the butter and combine with the milk, lemon, vanilla, and nutmeg in a medium-large mixing bowl.

3. Whisk in the eggs. Add the combined dry ingredients and the wild blueberries, stirring just to combine well.

4. Divide evenly and bake in the parchment lined muffin tins until puffed and golden. This will take approximately 20 minutes for mini-sized muffins; 25–30 minutes for full-sized muffins.

QUEEN OF THE GREEN QUICHE CUPS

MAKES 4 MINI QUICHES.

Fairies love all the fresh, green vegetables that grow so abundantly each spring and summer. And of course, they also love the color green! These fairy-sized little quiche cups form a self-crust of crunchy bread crumbs and a dense green center of yummy spinach. This makes 4 mini quiches, although if you are "fairy" hungry, it's easy to double the ingredients. (Just make sure you have enough custard cups!)

2 green onions

1 tablespoon olive oil

5 ounces chopped spinach (½ of a 10-ounce box of frozen, or use fresh if you prefer)

¼ teaspoon salt

6 grinds black pepper

⅛ teaspoon grated nutmeg

1 teaspoon dry parsley flakes

¼ teaspoon dried dill weed

4 teaspoons soft butter

4 tablespoons dry bread crumbs (Panko style works well)

½ cup shredded cheddar cheese

2 large eggs

½ cup small curd cottage cheese

½ cup milk

1. Wash and trim the green onions. Slice thinly. Preheat oven to 375°.

2. In a small heavy frying pan over medium heat, warm the olive oil. Add the sliced green onions and cook for a minute. Add in the spinach, salt, pepper, nutmeg, parsley, and dill weed, and sauté over medium heat until the spinach has lost all its moisture. Remove from the pan and set aside to cool to room temperature.

3. Butter four custard cups with one teaspoon of butter in each, smearing it generously around and up the sides. Sprinkle one tablespoon of the crumbs in each buttered custard cup, swirling them around to cover completely. Space the custard cups evenly in a 9x13-inch baking pan and set aside.

4. Combine the eggs, cottage cheese, and milk in a blender and blend until smooth (it's OK if a few small lumps of cottage cheese remain). Divide the cooled spinach mixture between the four custard cups. Top evenly with the cheddar cheese. Carefully pour the egg mixture over the top of each, making them as even as possible.

5. Bake for about 30 minutes, until the tops are puffed and just lightly browned. Allow to cool about 5 minutes before eating. Store any leftovers, covered, in the refrigerator and enjoy within 2 days.

Teatime in Fairyland

Teatime has been an important fairy tradition for many generations. The foods the fairies serve can be sweet or savory, and while they are generally dainty, larger items may occasionally also be enjoyed. Fairy tea services, such as cups, saucers, and spoons, vary depending on the fairy clan involved. Some woodland fairies prefer rustic cups made from nutshells. Meadow fairies frequently weave placemats and tablecloths from various grasses, embellishing them with wildflowers. The more established fairy families often have treasured tea sets of fine china, which are carefully handed down from fairy parents to fairy children. Whichever teacups they may use, the beverage of choice is almost always some type of tea, frequently brewed from plants the fairies have harvested. Mint leaves, rose hips, and elderflowers are all popular choices. The dairy fairies frequently are just as content to sip on a cool cup of milk, while garden and orchard fairies have been known to enjoy a wide variety of fruit juices. In addition to the teatime recipes included here, there are a number of sweet treats listed under *Fairy Dessert Delights* that could nicely enhance your next fairy tea party.

Open-Face Egg Flower Sandwiches

MAKES 1 SERVING.

In this recipe we are making one of the fairies' favorite foods, eggs, into sandwiches that look like flowers! The fairies particularly like them when they are made with blue colored eggs. They use red cabbage leaves to color the outer egg blue, and we have a recipe so that you can do this, too, if you wish. You may either toast the English muffin halves or leave them untoasted. Your sandwich will look neater if you cut the English muffins in half rather than pulling them apart.

1 English muffin, split
Soft butter or mayonnaise
1 hard-cooked, peeled egg, colored if you
    wish (see page 23)
Sea salt & pepper to taste
Celery leaves, or parsley sprigs, optional

1. Spread each half of the English muffin with your choice of mayonnaise or softened butter.

2. Carefully cut the egg in half horizontally and gently remove the two halves of the yolk. Set aside.

3. Now cut each half of the cooked white in half crossways. This will make your flower "petals" short enough to fit on the English muffin rounds.

4. Cut each of the four egg white sections into four evenly sized flower petal shapes. This will give you eight of them for each English muffin round. Arrange them like a wagon wheel, with the thinner ends pointing out, and place one of the yolk halves, flat side down, in the center.

5. Garnish your flower blossoms with celery leaves or parsley sprigs, if you wish, and season them to taste with salt and pepper.

Fairy Magic Colored Eggs

Even though eggs can easily be tinted with food coloring, the fairies prefer more natural coloring sources. This process can take a little longer than other methods, but the fairies find it much more fun to create their own coloring agents from fruits and vegetables. Who would think you could make such a pretty shade of blue using red cabbage leaves? The ingredients for each color are listed first, with directions for cooking and coloring the eggs at the end.

Robin's Egg Blue

Eggs colored in this solution may initially appear lavender colored. They will eventually turn a pretty blue, often after they have been removed from the coloring solution. They do take a bit longer to dye than some of the other egg colors.

3 cups shredded red cabbage
3 cups water
1 tablespoon white vinegar
Optional: ¼ teaspoon salt, 1 tablespoon sugar

Milkweed Blossom Mauve

2 medium sized red beets, scrubbed and
   cut into eighths
3 cups water
1 tablespoon white vinegar
Optional: 1 tablespoon sugar, ¼ teaspoon salt

Wild Violet Lavender

If desired, you can use 2¾ cups of grape juice in place of the red grapes and water, but note that it will yield a more blueish lavender, as shown in the picture on page 25.

3 cups seedless red grapes, well washed
2¾ cups water
1 tablespoon white vinegar
Optional: 1 tablespoon sugar, ¼ teaspoon
   salt

Golden Goose Yellow

2 cups shredded orange carrots
1 tablespoon white vinegar
½ teaspoon ground turmeric
Optional: 1 tablespoon sugar, ¼ teaspoon salt)

Ferny Green

Color the eggs using first the red cabbage mixture and then the carrot-turmeric mixture. They will turn a pretty shade of ferny green.

1. For each coloring solution, combine the preferred vegetable or fruit, the water, and the white vinegar in a medium-sized non-reactive saucepan. The salt and sugar are optional add-ins if you are coloring the eggs after they have been shelled; they will mellow out the flavors of the various fruits and vegetables used. The turmeric does impart a rather pronounced flavor; take this into consideration when deciding whether to color in or out of the shell.

2. Bring the solution(s) to a boil, lower the heat, and simmer, covered, for about 15 to 20 minutes. Cool and then transfer the entire mixture to glass jars or bowls for coloring the eggs (make sure you can fit them into your refrigerator)!

continued on next page

To hard-cook eggs:

1. Place eggs in medium saucepan and cover them with cool water. Cover the pan and bring just to a boil. Immediately turn off the heat and leave the eggs, tightly covered, for 10 minutes.

2. Pour off the hot water and run cold water over the eggs to cool the pan down. Then cover the eggs with fresh cold water and leave them for about 15 minutes to cool thoroughly.

3. If you prefer plain hard-cooked eggs, you may now refrigerate them, either in or out of their shells. Sometimes you may wish to color the eggs in their shells, which will work well with white shelled eggs, but not so much if they are brown shelled. If coloring them in the shell, the eggs can simply be submerged in the desired liquids and placed in the refrigerator for at least a few hours, or until the desired shade is reached.

4. For some recipes, you will need the shells off. If this is the case, crack the eggs at either end to make peeling them easier. Holding the egg under running water also helps to gently loosen the membrane (thin skin) that surrounds the cooked white. Gently peel the eggs, trying to keep them as smooth and intact as possible. Place in the desired, cold coloring solution, weighting them down if necessary, and leave in the refrigerator for up to 12 hours.

5. Some of the solutions will color the eggs more rapidly than others. Plan to use your hard-cooked eggs within a couple of days. (Note that the process of coloring the eggs without the shells may result in a slight toughening of the outer surface of the egg white. This is not harmful; just a slightly different texture when you are eating them.)

WILD VIOLET TEA SANDWICHES

MAKES AS MANY TEA SANDWICHES AS YOU WISH.

These little sandwiches are a springtime fairy specialty. They are usually served after the fairies have successfully harvested the many wild violet blossoms needed to make up a lovely batch of Wild Violet Jelly. There is a recipe included later in this book for how to concoct your own jelly from violets. However, if you don't have access to wild violets, or if it seems too daunting to try and pick so many of them, grape jelly makes a very nice substitute. A blossom-shaped cookie cutter works best for these, although other shapes can be cut out, too.

Slices of firm white or other favorite bread
Softened cream cheese
Wild Violet Jelly (page 76) or grape jelly
Fresh wild violet blossoms*, picked from a
    clean, pesticide-free source

*Please do not confuse wild violets with the potted houseplant called African violets. African violets are not edible!

1. For each tea sandwich, use a large cookie cutter to cut a blossom shape from a slice of the bread.

2. Carefully spread the bread with softened cream cheese. Place a spoonful of jelly in the center and arrange fresh violet blossoms decoratively around the edges. These are lovely served with lemonade, or a little cup of herbal tea.

Fairy Fancy Melon Stacks

MAKES AS MANY MELON STACKS AS YOU WISH.

Here is a perfect fairy treat for late summer, when melons are ripe and bursting with flavor. Cut the melons into thin slices and use small cookie cutters to form into a variety of shapes and sizes. Stack the fancy melon slices along with other desired small fruits, such as berries, cherries, grapes, and bits of kiwi or carambola. Anchor each upright stack with a tiny skewer or long wooden toothpick; about 3 or 4 inches is a good length. Soon you'll have fairies fluttering around them, hoping for a taste of sweet melon!

Seedless watermelon
Cantaloupe, either whole, half, or pre-sliced
   (not cubed)
Honeydew, either whole, half, or pre-sliced
   (not cubed)
Assorted berries and other small fruits,
   such as cherries, grapes, kiwi, star
   fruit, etc.
Wooden toothpicks or small wooden
   skewers

1. Look for sweet, ripe melons, but not overripe, especially if buying pre-sliced. Using a half or quarter of a whole seedless watermelon works well. Rinse the melons and dry the outer rinds.

2. Use a long, sharp knife and a large cutting board for best results. If the melon is pre-cut, slice a very thin layer from any of the pre-cut surfaces to ensure freshness. Slice the watermelon about ½ inch thick, removing the rind.

3. Now cut out a variety of shapes, starting with round or flower-shaped cutters about 2 inches in diameter. You will be able to cut larger shapes from the watermelon than from the other melons, but will also want some smaller shapes to add variety to the stacks. Now do the same with honeydew melon and the cantaloupe. Rinse and dry any berries you wish to use in your stacks. Smaller strawberries should be used; larger ones will dwarf the rest of the fruits in the stacks!

4. Now the fun begins! Place a larger sized watermelon cut-out on the serving plate. Add smaller melon cut-outs, varying colors and shapes as you go. Use a small wooden skewer or toothpick to anchor the stacked fruits. As you near the top of each stack, add in a berry or two, topping off with a tiny piece of fancy cut-out melon. A variety of stacks on a pretty serving platter makes a pleasing presentation; slide individual stacks off carefully onto individual serving plates.

Hummus Pinecones with Nutty Leaf Crackers

MAKES 2-3 DOZEN CRACKERS.

Deep in the densely wooded forests, woodland elves flit from branch to branch, their tiny lights twinkling in the dusky green. These fairies are extremely fond of nuts, and use them in many of their favorite dishes. Although actual pinecones are inedible, they do look very pretty on a dining table. It's fun to form your own "pinecone" from hummus, adding sliced almonds to give it that special, pinecone-y look. It's best to form each cone either on the serving platter, for larger cones, or individual plates for smaller ones, as the hummus is too soft to keep the cone shape otherwise. Serve it with nutty little leaf-shaped crackers made from pine nuts, the edible seeds harvested from the cones of some pine trees. If you prefer, the crackers may also be made with almonds, another tasty tree nut the fairies are quite fond of.

Favorite flavor of hummus; 2 or more
    tablespoons per cone
Sliced almonds, lightly toasted if you wish

Nutty Leaf Crackers
¼ cup pine nuts (slivered almonds may be
    substituted, if you wish)
½ cup all-purpose flour
¼ cup whole wheat flour
½ teaspoon garlic salt or ¼ teaspoon sea
    salt
½ teaspoon crushed dried rosemary
4 tablespoons coconut oil
4 tablespoons cold water

1. Whirl the nuts in a blender or food processor until they are finely ground.

2. Combine the ground nuts in a medium mixing bowl with the all-purpose flour, whole wheat flour, garlic salt or sea salt, and rosemary, stirring to mix well.

3. Add the coconut oil in 4 or more pieces to facilitate even blending. Now, either with your fingers, or by again using the blender or food processor, work the mixture to fine crumbs.

4. Return to the bowl and sprinkle the cold water over the top. Work it in gently with a fork or your fingers; the dough should come together nicely but will still be a little crumbly. Form into a smooth ball, or divide in half for easier rolling.

5. Place your oven rack in an upper position in the oven. Preheat oven to 375°.

6. Roll the dough out on an even, lightly floured surface to about ¹⁄₁₆ of an inch thickness. You want the crackers to be thin and crispy once they are baked. Cut with a lightly floured cookie cutter and place about an inch apart on an ungreased baking sheet. Lightly prick the top of each with a fork.

7. Bake for approximately 12–14 minutes, until the outer edges are lightly browned. Remove from oven and carefully place on wire racks to cool. To make the "pinecones," center the desired amount of hummus on a plate and form into a cone shape. Carefully insert concentric rows of sliced almonds so that it has that distinctive, pinecone look. Arrange the Nutty Leaf Crackers around it and enjoy!

Broccoli Grove Sandwich Crisps

MAKES AS MANY SANDWICH CRISPS AS YOU WISH.

As we've mentioned previously, fairies being much smaller folk than humans, frequently have a different perspective on the fruits and vegetables they grow and harvest than we might. For instance, the fairies farm broccoli in groves similar to how we might cultivate fruit and nut trees. When it's time for the broccoli harvest, shouts of *"Tim-ber!"* ring through the crisp fall air, as each broccoli tree crashes to the ground. The industrious fairies make short work of cutting up the broccoli into manageable pieces before hauling it back to their fairy homes, to be enjoyed fresh or frozen for future meals. These open-face broccoli snacks feature crispy rye crackers spread with cream cheese and then topped lavishly with broccoli "trees," sunflower seeds, and whatever other bits of tastiness you might enjoy.

Rectangular rye crisp crackers (whole graham crackers may be substituted for fairies with a sweet tooth; these will taste better when spread with cream cheese rather than hummus)

Soft spread cream cheese

Hummus, optional

Blue gel food coloring, optional

Blueberry Fruited Fairy Dust (page 117), optional

Broccoli florets, thinly sliced

Hulled sunflower seeds

Fresh parsley, dill weed, and/or basil leaves, optional

Assorted small veggies cut in flower or star shapes, as you wish

Assorted dried fruits, to form flowers and/or stars, as you wish

1. The broccoli for these crisps can either be enjoyed raw, or blanched slightly to mellow out the flavor and enhance the bright green color. If you wish to blanch the broccoli, trim and slice it into pieces. Heat a medium-sized pan of water to boiling. Add the broccoli and leave it in the water until it just comes to a boil again. Now drain the broccoli and submerge it in cold water to stop the cooking process. Pat the drained broccoli with paper towels to remove excess water before constructing the crisps.

2. Spread each piece of rye crisp with a thin layer of cream cheese, placing them length-wise on your work surface. If you prefer, you can spread cream cheese on top and use hummus for the ground underneath. Squirt just a dab of the blue gel food coloring on the top half of one cream cheese-coated piece and spread it back and forth horizontally to create a pretty blue sky. Repeat with the other pieces. As an alternative, you can omit the gel and sprinkle a bit of blueberry Fruited Fairy Dust on the top half of each crisp, although the color won't be as vibrant.

3. Add two or three broccoli "trees" to each crisp and sprinkle a few sunflower seeds around their bases. Add in whatever additional herbs, fruits, and/or vegetables you would like. Serve them as soon as possible, so that your crisps remain crisp! This will make as many Broccoli Grove Sandwich Crisps as you wish.

Cheesy Pixie Puffs

MAKES 12 PUFFS.

The pixies' farmyard cousins, the dairy fairies, often are willing to contribute cheese, butter, and eggs in return for a few of these special, savory treats. The little puffs bake up light and airy in the oven and are frequently enjoyed warm with soup, although they are also quite delicious all by themselves. The higher gluten content in the bread flour helps create crispy, crunchy exteriors on the puffs.

¼ cup water
¼ cup milk
¼ cup butter
¼ teaspoon paprika
½ teaspoon salt
½ cup bread flour
2 large eggs
¾ cup shredded cheese such as Monterey Jack or mild cheddar
Poppy seeds, sesame seeds, or "everything" topping, optional

1. Place the oven rack in the middle position and preheat the oven to 400°. Line a large baking sheet with parchment paper.

2. In a small saucepan, combine the water, milk, butter, paprika, and salt. Bring to a boil over medium heat and then carefully stir in the flour all at once; a wooden spoon or heatproof spatula works well for this. Continue to cook for about a minute longer; the mixture will firm up and form a ball. Remove from the heat.

3. Beat in each egg, one at a time, stirring vigorously to combine well. Allow the mixture to cool just slightly, for a couple of minutes, before stirring in the shredded cheese. Carefully drop in 12 even mounds on the parchment-lined baking sheet. A small scoop works well for this, or a smaller sized spoon.

4. Bake for about 35 minutes, until they are puffed up and golden. Although you do not want them to burn, it is also important not to under-bake them, or they may lose their puffiness! Allowing them to remain in the oven for a few minutes after it has been turned off, with the door slightly open, helps ensure stability. Pixie Puffs are very yummy served while they are still warm, although they are also tasty at room temperature. If you need to save any for another day, store them, covered, in the refrigerator.

Brownies' Brownies

MAKES 16 SMALL BROWNIES.

The fairies find this recipe title quite amusing, for it reminds them of their distant cousins who live mostly in Scotland and England. Brownies, a bit wilder than the average fairy, come out only at night and will frequently help protect farm animals, or even birds and beasts living on the moors, as long as they are kept happy with a bit of milk and honey. The fairies think they'd be even happier with some of these chewy, gooey brownies to go with their glasses of milk! If you wish, you can decorate the tops of your brownies with berries or nuts to make them even more festive.

⅓ cup dark cocoa powder
⅔ cup all-purpose flour
½ teaspoon salt
1¼ cups sugar
2 large eggs
⅓ cup corn oil (or other liquid
  vegetable oil)
¼ cup water
½ teaspoon vanilla extract
½ cup chopped walnuts or hazelnuts,
  optional
Berries, cherries, or nut halves for garnish,
  optional
Chocolate hazelnut spread for attaching the
  garnish, optional

1. Adjust baking rack to middle position. Preheat oven to 350°.

2. Combine all the dry ingredients in a medium mixing bowl. Add the eggs, oil, water, and vanilla, stirring to combine well. Stir in the nuts, if you are using them.

3. Spread in a greased and floured 9x9-inch baking pan. Bake for approximately 30 minutes, until top is glossy and puffed but brownies are not totally set. Allow the brownies to cool before cutting them into 16 petite pieces.

4. To garnish them, place about ½ teaspoon of the chocolate hazelnut spread in the middle of each brownie and then place a nut half, raspberry, cherry, or small strawberry on top of the spread. Brownies topped with fruit should be stored in the refrigerator, although nut topped or plain are fine stored at room temperature. Just be sure to cover them securely to keep them fresh.

CRESCENT MOON COOKIE CUPS

MAKES 12 COOKIE CUPS.

Fairies are fond of mathematics. They enjoy predicting how many baby bunnies will be born each year in the spring woods, or noticing the sequences in the spirals of acorn caps and pinecones. (A famous mathematician named Fibonacci gave them some really helpful guidelines.) These cookie cups are quite easy to make, mathematically speaking, because almost everything in them is measured by halves or quarters. However, the sweet clementine slices on top can be any fraction of the fruit you wish them to be. You will be baking these cookies in a muffin tin; each muffin cup will be about half full of cookie dough when you place them in the oven.

½ cup (1 stick) butter, softened
1 cup lightly packed dark brown sugar
½ teaspoon pure vanilla extract
½ teaspoon natural orange flavoring
1 large egg
½ cup all-purpose flour
¼ cup whole wheat flour
¼ cup quick-cooking rolled oats
½ teaspoon baking soda
½ teaspoon salt
¼ cup chopped pistachios or chopped
   pecans
¼ cup dried cranberries
¼ cup semi-sweet chocolate chips

Glaze
¼ cup cream
½ cup semi-sweet chocolate chips
Fresh clementine segments (although
   the fairies prefer fresh fruits, canned
   mandarin orange sections, well drained,
   may be substituted in a pinch)

1. First prepare your muffin tin. This recipe makes 12 cookie cups, so you will need either a 12-cup tin or two 6-cup tins. Either line them with parchment cupcake holders or spray regular paper cupcake liners well with non-stick cooking spray so that you can lift the cookie cups out easily when they are cool.

2. In a large mixing bowl using the paddle attachment of the mixer, cream together the butter, brown sugar, and flavorings until they are light and fluffy. Add the egg and mix until combined. You can also beat them together with a wooden spoon if you don't have a mixer; it is a great way to build up your mighty muscles!

3. Stir in the combined flours, rolled oats, baking soda, and salt until the dough is smooth and creamy. Lastly stir in the pistachios, dried cranberries, and the ¼ cup of semi-sweet chocolate chips.

4. Scoop the dough evenly into the muffin cups. Bake for about 12 minutes, until the cookies are lightly browned around the edges but still soft in the middle. Allow the cookie cups to cool completely before carefully removing, with the liners, from the muffin tin; otherwise they may break apart.

5. Make the glaze by heating the cream in a small saucepan until it just begins to boil (bubbles will form

continued on next page

around the edge of the pan). Remove from the heat and sprinkle the chocolate chips evenly into the hot cream. Allow this mixture to sit for about a minute, to soften the chocolate, and then stir the cream and chocolate together until it's nice and smooth. The cookie cups should have a slightly depressed area in the center; spoon a bit of the chocolate glaze into each of the cookie cups, smoothing gently. Just before serving, top each with one clementine segment. (The fairies enjoy placing one segment because it reminds them of a crescent moon, although more bits of clementine are even tastier to eat!) Refrigerate any leftovers to enjoy another day.

Rings of Roses

MAKES 12 RINGS.

This hand-formed cookie is based on a very old recipe, handed down from the great-great-grandfairies to present day. It features rose water and rose petals, favorites of the fairies, with just a hint of spice added in. If you love rose essence, use the full amount of rose water in the icing. Alternatively, combining half rose water and half lemon juice produces a lighter rose flavor with a hint of tangy lemon. The little ring cookies look very pretty, with their sweet icing and dusting of rose petals, arranged on a delicate serving tray. Served with a pot of hot tea, they are just perfect for a fairy tea party.

¼ cup soft butter
½ cup confectioner's sugar
1 egg
1 teaspoon rose water
1 cup all-purpose flour
¼ teaspoon nutmeg
¼ teaspoon cinnamon

Glaze
1 cup confectioner's sugar
1 teaspoon lemon juice and 1 teaspoon
    rose water or 2 teaspoons rose water
Fresh, dried, or sugared rose petals

1. Move oven racks to the middle and upper positions. Preheat the oven to 375°.

2. Cream together the butter and confectioner's sugar in a medium-sized bowl. Add the egg and rose water and cream again, until the mixture is light and fluffy.

3. Now carefully stir in the combined flour, nutmeg, and cinnamon to form a pliable dough. Pinch off bits of the dough to form 12 evenly sized portions. Roll each piece of dough between your palms to form a rope about 6 inches long. Coil into a circle with a hole in the center on a parchment-lined baking sheet; pinch the ends together to join smoothly.

4. Bake for 8–10 minutes, until firm; the undersides may be lightly browned but the tops will still be pale. Loosen the cookies on the sheet without removing them (they will break apart while still hot) and allow to cool thoroughly. Combine the rose water, lemon juice if using, and confectioner's sugar in a small bowl. Add just a few drops of water if needed; the icing should be of a thick pouring consistency.

5. Dip the top of each cookie to glaze evenly. Decorate with bits of rose petals; allow the icing to set before serving.

Pastel Berry Shortbread Rounds

MAKES 24 SHORTBREAD ROUNDS.

These dainty shortbread cookies are much loved by fairies. The fruitiness of the fairy dust adds a pleasing flavor, while the colors of the powdered berries give the cookies a pretty, speckled look. Blueberry or raspberry fairy dust give the cookies a particularly nice flavor. The fairies enjoy their Pastel Berry Shortbread Rounds with a cup of herbal tea, or possibly a mug of steaming cocoa. Store your little shortbreads in airtight containers to keep them fresh and crisp.

1 cup soft butter
¾ cup confectioner's sugar
3 tablespoons berry based Fruited Fairy
    Dust (page 117), divided
2 cups all-purpose flour
¼ cup granulated sugar

1. Cream together the butter, confectioner's sugar, and 2 tablespoons of the Fruited Fairy Dust until light and fluffy. Carefully stir in the flour. The dough will seem crumbly at first, but will eventually come together into a ball.

2. In a small bowl, combine the remaining tablespoon of the fairy dust with the granulated sugar, stirring to mix well.

3. Using a piece of waxed paper, plastic wrap, or parchment paper, sprinkle the fruited sugar in a line about 2 inches wide and 12 inches long, just off-center. You can do two different colors if you wish, as shown in the picture to the left. Form the dough into a roll about 2 inches in diameter and 12 inches long. Roll the dough back and forth in the fruited sugar to coat the entire outside of the roll. Wrap the coated dough roll completely in the paper, twisting the ends shut. Place on a level surface in the fridge to chill completely; at least one hour or up to a few days.

4. When ready to bake, adjust the oven racks to middle and upper positions and preheat the oven to 350°. Unwrap the chilled dough and place it on a cutting board. Slice the dough into thin rounds and place on parchment-lined baking sheets. Bake for approximately 8 minutes, until the rounds are lightly browned around the edges but still quite pale.

5. Carefully loosen the shortbread rounds; they are fragile when hot. After a minute or so, transfer them to wire racks to complete cooling.

Rainbow Tea Bread

MAKES 1 LOAF.

Rainbows are much loved of water fairies. Actually, most fairies enjoy viewing a rainbow; sometimes they will even fly up to try and find its beginning! Now you can view a rainbow whenever you'd like; and enjoy eating it, too! You will need two 6-inch round, deep cake tins to bake this pretty tri-colored bread. Once it's cooled, it can be sliced into lovely little rainbows and enjoyed as a sandwich, or even just spread with a bit of butter. It also makes delightful Rainbow-in-the-Clouds French Toast (page 14), a special breakfast, lunch, or brunch treat.

½ cup milk
2 tablespoons butter
½ cup warm water
2 tablespoons honey
¾ teaspoon salt
1 tablespoon active dry yeast
Approximately 3 cups bread flour
Red, blue, and yellow gel food coloring
Non-stick cooking spray *or* extra butter

1. Warm the milk and butter together just until the butter melts. Remove from the heat and pour into a large mixing bowl. Stir in the warm water, honey, and salt. At this point the liquid should be pleasantly warm, but not hot. Sprinkle the yeast over the top and stir to dissolve.

2. Mix in 1½ cups of the flour, stirring it vigorously to form a batter. The fairies have found that the easiest way to color the bread is to divide the batter now, before adding the rest of the flour. Measure ⅓ cup of the bread batter into a small mixing bowl. Measure ½ cup of the batter into another mixing bowl. Keep the rest of the batter in the original bowl. Add a few drops of blue coloring gel to the smallest bowl of batter, a few drops of yellow to the second bowl of batter, and a few drops of red gel to the larger bowl of batter,

mixing each in well, being sure to use different spoons for each. Tint the batters fairly deep pastel shades, as adding more flour and then baking the bread will lighten them up a bit.

3. Now add ½ cup flour to the pink bowl of batter, ¼ cup of flour to the yellow batter, and 3 tablespoons to the blue batter. Cover and allow to rise in a warm, moist place for about 1 hour, until the mounds of dough appear twice as big (we call this "doubled in bulk").

4. Turn each colored mound of dough, one at a time, out on a lightly floured, clean, smooth surface. Knead the dough with your hands (pushing and rolling it back and forth) until it becomes smooth and elastic feeling, adding only a bit of flour to help prevent sticking, if you need to. This is good exercise for your hands, and will make your bread nice and light!

5. Allow the dough to "rest" while you spray each baking pan generously with non-stick spray (or you may use your fingers to smear soft butter all over the insides of the pans, if you prefer).

6. Now divide each color of dough in half. Roll each half of the pink dough into a thin, 18-inch rope. Coil each around the inside of one prepared pan to form a ring, pushing it against the edge and making sure the two ends are pinched firmly together. Roll out each yellow half into a 14-inch coil and form a slightly smaller ring just inside

continued on next page

the pink one, again pinching the ends. Finally form each blue dough half into a smooth ball and place in the middle of the dough rings in each pan, pressing it down slightly. Allow the bread to rise again, in a warm, moist area for about 45 minutes, until it is puffed up and slightly mounded, but the outer rings have not quite come up over edges of the pan.

7. Bake in a preheated 350° oven for about 25 minutes, until the bread sounds hollow when tapped and the bottom is lightly browned. Gently remove from pans and place upright on wire rack to cool completely before slicing. Placing the cooled bread in the refrigerator for an hour or two to chill will make slicing it even easier.

8. Carefully cut each bread round into two even half circles. Each half will now resemble a rainbow that you can stand upright on the cut end. Cut a very thin slice off the bottom crust and the top of the bread where it may have become slightly domed while baking. You will now have a pretty rainbow peeking out at you! Carefully cut down through each little rainbow to make 4 thin slices of rainbow bread; eight in all per pan of bread. Gently wrap any leftovers in plastic to stay fresh for another day. The slices can also be frozen. Don't forget to enjoy the scraps you've trimmed from the bread; they are a little bonus for the baker!

Looks-Like-a-Mushroom Oat and Honey Bread

MAKES 1 LOAF.

This recipe may have come from the brownies, those Celtic counterparts of our North American fairies who live in the Irish and Scottish countryside. The wild bees they befriend provide plenty of sweet golden honey for this yummy round bread made with rolled oats and sunflower seeds. Honey and whole wheat flour make this round little loaf of bread irresistible to hungry fairies! They can't wait to slather soft butter on the warm slices!

1 cup milk
¼ cup butter
¾ teaspoon salt
½ cup quick-cooking rolled oats
¼ cup honey
1 tablespoon dry yeast
½ cup whole wheat flour
2 cups unbleached bread flour
¼ cup + 2 tablespoons hulled sunflower
  seeds

1. In a large, heatproof bowl or saucepan, combine the milk, butter, and salt. Warm this mixture until the butter melts. Remove from the heat and stir in the rolled oats and honey. Allow this to cool until it is lukewarm; not too hot and not too cold.

2. Stir in the yeast and whole wheat flour and allow to rest for about 5 minutes, so that the yeast begins to bubble. Stir in the bread flour, 1 cup at a time. Add the sunflower seeds with the second cup of flour and stir to combine very well. You should now have a fairly stiff dough that feels just slightly sticky.

3. Cover the bowl and allow the dough to rise in a warm, undisturbed place for about 45 minutes, until it has doubled in size. Meanwhile, generously butter a deep, 6-inch round cake pan.

4. When the dough has doubled, butter your hands, remove the dough from the bowl, and gently form it into a ball; fit it into the buttered pan. Allow it to rise, loosely covered, for another ½ hour. While it is rising, preheat the oven to 350°.

5. Once the dough has risen almost over the top of the pan, bake in the preheated oven for 35–40 minutes, until it is deep golden brown and sounds hollow when tapped on top. The baked bread should now resemble a big, brown mushroom. Brush the top lightly with butter, if you wish, and allow to cool in the pan for about 10 minutes. Then carefully tip the bread out of the pan and place it upright on a wire rack until it has totally cooled. This is very tasty served with butter and perhaps a little extra honey. Wrap any leftovers airtight to store.

BROWNIES' BIRTHDAY BREAD

MAKES 1 LOAF.

Sometimes when very patient, a lucky brownie is rewarded with a special decorated loaf of bread that looks like a cake. Soft spread cream cheese forms the frosting. It is then lavishly adorned with lovely flowers made from vegetables and herbs, creating a decorated round bread fit for a fairy feast (or a brownie birthday!). If you're in a hurry, any six-inch round loaf may be substituted for the oat and honey bread.

1 loaf Looks-Like-a-Mushroom Oat and Honey Bread (page 47)
16 ounces soft spread cream cheese (not whipped)
Shredded and sliced rainbow carrots (purple, orange, and yellow)
Thinly sliced radishes
Parsley, dill, basil, and/or celery sprigs or leaves
Zucchini slices or green pepper strips

1. Trim a large, flat slice off the top of the loaf, if you wish, so that it will sit flat and you have a smooth, cake-like surface to work with. If you prefer to keep the mushroom shape, simply leave the bread standing on its base. It will be a little more challenging to frost if left this way, but will look very pretty. Frost the entire exterior of the bread with the soft spread cream cheese.

2. Now the fun begins! Place halved radish slices in circles to form flowers, placing a small slice of rainbow carrot in the center of each. Arrange shredded carrots in a sunburst circular pattern, using a different color for each "flower." Center a contrasting slice of carrot in the middle of each. Cut thin edges from zucchini slices to form leaves, or cut leaf shapes from green peppers, if you prefer. Garnish all with the various herbs. Other vegetables may be added if you wish; halved cherry or grape tomatoes in a variety of colors make nice additions.

3. Chill the birthday bread until you're ready to slice and serve it. Feel free to add lighted candles, if you wish!

FAIRIES' FAVORITE COMPANION CRITTERS

MAKES AS MANY CRITTERS AS YOU WISH.

There are so many tiny creatures inhabiting the meadows and woodlands that we never even see! The fairies, of course, know them all. Since we're not really sure what a lot of these little beasts look like, it's a grand time to use our imaginations to create some of our own from a variety of fresh veggies. Dabs of cream cheese, hummus, or peanut butter help hold them together, with an occasional toothpick or mini skewer to stabilize the larger critters. Dried fruits, olives, and capers add the finishing touches to these tasty little companions. Here are just a few suggestions; feel free to create your own!

Whole, sliced, and shredded rainbow
   carrots
Celery stalks
Whole radishes
Small cucumbers
Snow peas or sugar pod peas
Bell peppers in a variety of colors
Soft spread cream cheese and/or hummus
   and/or peanut butter
Stuffed olives, large and small
Capers
Dried blueberries
Golden raisins
Dried cranberries
Cherry tomatoes

Hopper: Use a short length of carrot, flattened on one side, for the base. Cut the leaf end from a small radish, skewer the radish with a wooden toothpick, and insert it into the carrot for the critter's head. The radish's root will form a little nose. Pipe cream cheese, hummus, or peanut butter along the length of the carrot, fastening a snow pea onto either side. Alternate thin slices of celery and stuffed olives down the back. Place two small dabs of cheese, hummus, or peanut butter on the radish head, adding capers or dried blueberries for eyes.

Wiggly Caterpillar: Attach a variety of similarly sized cherry tomatoes together with a short wooden skewer. Piercing some of them slightly off-center will make the caterpillar look as though it's wiggling. Add a large, stuffed olive to one end, with the olive's open "mouth" showing the pimento stuffing like a little caterpillar tongue searching for a flower to eat! Dabs of cream cheese, hummus, or peanut butter on the olive will hold capers or dried blueberries in place for eyes to find that flower.

Baby Caterpillar: Use a short length of celery. Trim a little off the curved back, so that it will sit flat for you. Pipe cream cheese or peanut butter along the length of the celery. Alternate dried cranberries and golden raisins down the caterpillar's length. Add two tiny dabs of cheese or peanut butter to one end and affix two dried blueberries for baby caterpillar eyes.

LUNCHEON & DINNER DELICACIES

Fairies love to snack throughout the day, sipping on nectar from flowers or sampling bits of fruits and veggies from their many gardens. However, they also appreciate light but nourishing noontime and evening meals. Depending on the weather and the time of year, you might find them enjoying a crisp, cool salad or a warm, comforting bowl of soup. One of their favorite year-round foods, somewhat surprisingly, is pizza! Interestingly, many of them do not use the red tomato sauce we are used to. The fairies enjoy both savory and sweet variations topped, of course, with fresh seasonal fruits or vegetables.

Garden Delight White Pizza

MAKES TWO 9-INCH PIZZAS.

In this recipe, the dairy fairies and garden fairies have joined together to create a delicious summertime treat! Unlike many pizzas, the herbs for Garden Delight White Pizza are in the crust and drizzled over the toppings. And the tomatoes are fresh sliced, right from the fairies' gardens! As with all the fairy pizza recipes, Garden Delight White Pizza is baked in 9-inch cake pans, rather than the larger sized pizza pans we're more used to. The crusts are a bit thicker than some, making it easier to pick slices up with your fingers to enjoy. You'll also need your fingers to evenly distribute the cheesy toppings that make Garden Delight White Pizza a unique treat.

1 teaspoon dried Italian mixed herbs
2 teaspoons finely minced garlic, about 1 clove
¼ cup olive oil, plus extra for oiling the pans
1 cup very warm water + 1 tablespoon, divided
1 teaspoon sugar or honey
1 teaspoon sea salt
1 tablespoon active dry yeast
2¼–2½ cups all-purpose flour

Toppings
1 cup shredded mozzarella cheese
1 cup ricotta cheese
Thinly sliced fresh tomatoes
Finely cut strips of fresh basil leaves, or whole small basil leaves
Sea salt and fresh black pepper, if you wish
¼ cup shredded Parmesan cheese

1. Adjust oven racks to middle or lower positions and preheat the oven to 400°.

2. Combine the mixed herbs and garlic in a small saucepan. Add the tablespoon of warm water and allow the herbs to absorb a bit of it. Add in the olive oil and heat the mixture just long enough to soften but not brown the garlic. Remove from heat and set aside.

3. Combine the warm water, sugar or honey, salt, and 1 tablespoon of the garlic olive oil mixture in a large mixing bowl. Add in the yeast, stirring to dissolve, and then stir in the flour to form a soft but not-too-sticky dough.

4. Pour a little olive oil into each of two 9-inch round cake tins and spread it around with your fingers to coat the bottom of the pans. Lightly oil your fingers/hands and form the dough into two rounds. Place one round in each of the pans, pushing it gently to evenly cover the entire base.

5. Bake the crusts for about 8 minutes, until just firm but not browned. Sprinkle the mozzarella evenly over the tops of each. Using your fingers, pinch little bits of ricotta and place all over the mozzarella. Arrange slices of tomatoes over this and sprinkle with the basil. Drizzle everything with the reserved oil and garlic mixture. Season with a pinch or two of sea salt, and grind on a bit of black pepper, if you like. Top with the Parmesan cheese.

6. Return to the oven and bake for 15–20 minutes longer, until the cheeses are nicely melted and the tomatoes have lost most of their moisture. Allow to cool a few minutes before slicing into 4–6 wedges per pan.

Pear and Hazelnut Pizza

MAKES ONE 9-INCH PIZZA.

Hazelnuts, pears, and a bit of chocolate make this sweet pizza a fall fairy favorite! This is a grand harvest time treat, when nuts and pears are both ripe. The fairies also enjoy it during the winter, often as a part of their special holiday meals. (Hint: Fairies have also been known to enjoy this treat made with sliced apple rather than pear.) Because this is such a rich pizza, the directions make just one 9-inch round. Simply double the ingredients if you'd like more (and who wouldn't?).

½ cup very warm water
2 teaspoons sugar
¼ teaspoon sea salt
2 teaspoons active dry yeast
1 cup all-purpose flour
1 tablespoon olive oil
3 tablespoons ground toasted hazelnuts
1 tablespoon sugar
¼ cup chocolate hazelnut spread
1 fresh pear, slightly firm (red skinned is especially nice), washed, cored, and thinly sliced

1. Combine the warm water, 2 teaspoons sugar, and ¼ teaspoon salt. Sprinkle the yeast over the surface; stir to dissolve. Stir in the flour, ½ cup at a time. Allow the pizza dough to rest while you preheat the oven to 425°.

2. Pour the olive oil into a 9-inch round metal cake tin, spreading it around to coat the entire surface evenly. Place the dough in the pan, turning it to coat on all sides. Gently push and pull the dough to fit the pan, forming a slightly raised outer edge all the way around. Combine the ground hazelnuts and 1 tablespoon of sugar and sprinkle all over the surface of the dough.

3. Bake on an upper rack of the preheated oven for about 12–14 minutes, until it appears golden brown around the edges and feels firm to light touch. Remove from oven and place spoonfuls of the chocolate hazelnut spread on the hot crust. As it softens from the heat, gently spread it over the surface, leaving a plain rim around the edges. The ground hazelnut mixture will probably mix in with the spread a little bit and this is fine.

4. Place thin slices of the pear in concentric circles around the pizza, starting at the outer edge and working in. It will look almost like a rose in bloom, which will make the fairies very happy! It will be easier to cut the pizza if it is carefully removed to a cutting board first. Use a pizza cutter or sharp knife to cut into 4–8 even wedges and enjoy warm or cool. Refrigerate leftovers, covered lightly.

Elves' Emerald Mushroom Pizza

MAKES TWO 9-INCH PIZZAS.

When mushrooms and nuts are ready to be harvested in the woodlands, the elves and other forest fairies can once again enjoy their favorite mushroom pizza. They combine garden-fresh basil with nuts and other good things to make the bright green pesto topping for this unusual treat. They recommend using either baby portabella or white button mushrooms for this, as harvesting mushrooms in the forest is something only mushroom experts or woodland fairies should do (some wild mushrooms are poisonous!).

Pesto
2 cups loosely packed fresh basil leaves (not stems)
1–2 cloves fresh garlic, depending on size of garlic and the flavor you prefer
½ cup olive oil
¼ cup pine nuts or walnuts
½ teaspoon sea salt
½ cup finely shredded Parmesan cheese
1 teaspoon lemon juice, optional

Crust
¾ cup very warm water
1 teaspoon sea salt
1 teaspoon honey or maple syrup
1 tablespoon active dry yeast
½ cup whole wheat flour, optional
1½ cups all-purpose flour; increase to 2 cups if omitting the whole wheat flour
Olive oil for oiling the pans

Topping
4 ounces button mushrooms, rinsed and wiped dry, sliced
1 tablespoon olive oil
1 cup shredded mozzarella cheese

1. In a blender or food processor, whirl together all the pesto ingredients except the Parmesan cheese and lemon juice. Scrape into a small bowl and stir in the cheese by hand, adding lemon juice if you wish. Although it's not a traditional pesto ingredient, the lemon juice adds a nice bright flavor and also helps keep the pesto a vibrant green. Set the pesto aside, or cover tightly and refrigerate overnight.

2. When ready to bake your pizzas, preheat the oven to 450°. Combine the water, salt, and honey or maple syrup in a medium-large bowl. Stir in the yeast and ½ cup whole wheat (or all-purpose) flour until it forms a smooth batter. Allow the batter to rest for about 5 minutes so that the yeast has a chance to begin to work (form bubbles).

3. Beat in 1 cup of the all-purpose flour and then gradually add the rest, kneading with your hands if the dough becomes too stiff to stir with a spoon.

4. Generously apply olive oil to two 9-inch round cake pans. Divide the dough in half and form each into a round, gently pulling and stretching to fit in each pan. Spread some of the pesto over each to form a smooth green surface.

5. Toss the sliced mushrooms with the 1 tablespoon of olive oil to coat evenly and arrange in concentric circles on each pizza. Sprinkle with the shredded mozzarella. Bake on a middle rack: one pan for 13–15 minutes, two pans for a minute or two longer. The cheese should just be bubbling but not overly browned. Makes two 9-inch pizzas; 4–6 fairy-sized slices from each.

Flower Garden Salad

MAKES ¼ CUP DRESSING AND AS MUCH SALAD AS YOU WISH.

Salad is a favorite fairy food. Beginning in spring and early summer, tender leaf lettuce, rosy red radishes, and the first edible blossoms are ready to fill salad bowls. By midsummer, cucumbers, fresh herbs, and summer blooming flowers add to the mix. Flower Garden Salad features just a few fresh ingredients that combine into a light and pleasant dish. Garden fairies, and especially flower fairies, love gathering the salad fixings and concocting sweet tart salad dressing featuring lemon juice and golden honey. These salads are pretty as a picture, featuring whichever fresh, edible flowers strike your fairy fancy. Perhaps a Fondant Honeybee (page 123) will alight on one of the bowls!

Tender leaf lettuces
Thinly sliced radishes and/or cucumbers
Fresh edible flowers such as nasturtium,
    calendula, violet, bachelor's button,
    borage, rose

Honey Lemon Dressing

2 tablespoons honey
2 tablespoons lemon juice
¼ teaspoon salt
¼ cup olive oil
1 teaspoon finely minced fresh mint leaves,
    optional

1. Whisk together all the dressing ingredients in a small bowl. Pour into a cruet or small pitcher, if you wish.

2. Tear the lettuce into bite-sized pieces and place some in each individual salad bowl. Arrange the sliced radishes and/or cucumbers over the lettuce and sprinkle the flowers pleasingly over all. Although some fairies (and people) prefer the flowers just as a garnish, others enjoy sampling the different tastes and textures; some are spicier than others. Gently drizzle on the dressing just before enjoying your salad.

Frozen Fruit Salad

MAKES 12 SERVINGS.

Sometimes there are so many delicious summer fruits and berries available at the same time that the fairies don't quite know what to do with them all! Frozen Fruit Salad is a grand way to combine several different fruits with mellow cream cheese and whipped cream to produce a salad so fruity and creamy that you may even have it for dessert, if you prefer. The fairies have discovered that canned peaches freeze better than fresh for this recipe, probably because cooking in sweetened syrup has changed their texture. Feel free to experiment with other fruits, if you wish; just remember to cut them in tiny pieces, as they will harden when frozen.

2 individual serving size (4 ounce) cups diced juice-pack peaches

8-ounce can juice-pack crushed pineapple

½ cup sweet cherries, washed, pitted, and cut in fourths

½ cup small seedless green grapes, well washed and cut in half

¼ cup chopped pecans

4 ounces cream cheese, softened

½ teaspoon vanilla extract

⅛ teaspoon salt

½ cup confectioner's sugar

1 tablespoon lemon juice

1 cup heavy cream

1. Drain the peaches very well; you should have about ¾ cup of them. Drain the crushed pineapple very well and place in a separate bowl or measuring cup. (It's fine to combine the fruit juices; they are not needed in this recipe, but adding a little sparkling water will produce a refreshing beverage.)

2. Prepare the cherries and grapes and add them to the peaches; chop the pecans and add them as well.

3. Place the softened cream cheese in a medium mixing bowl. Add the vanilla, salt, confectioner's sugar, and lemon juice and beat until smooth and creamy. Add the crushed pineapple and beat again.

4. Beat the heavy cream to soft peaks before gently folding it into the cream cheese mixture. Lightly fold in the combined fruits and pecans until everything is well blended.

5. Divide the fruit salad mixture between 12 cupcake paper lined muffin cups. Freeze until firm; at least 2 hours. Cover the surfaces of the frozen salad cups to help keep them fresher. Serve them on a pretty plate or dish, still in the cupcake wrapper. Garnish with more fresh fruits or berries just before serving, if you wish. Plan to enjoy your Frozen Fruit Salad within a week or so for best results.

Water Nymphs' Bubble Bowl

MAKES 8 SERVINGS.

Splashing in the bubbles of a cool, clear pool—what could be more fun for a water nymph? The blue of the sky and green of the ferns surrounding the pool are reflected in this pretty, layered bubble bowl. Use a clear bowl to show off the colors and the grape "bubbles," or if you prefer, the gelatin and grapes can be layered in a ring mold, to form a bubble ring! Either way, it's easy to prepare and fun to eat.

1 packet blueberry-flavored gelatin powder
1 packet lime-flavored gelatin powder
2–3 cups seedless green grapes
2 cups apple juice or white grape juice, optional
2–4 cups water, depending on whether you use juice for part of the liquid

1. You will need two medium-sized saucepans for the two kinds of gelatin, or alternatively an extra bowl to temporarily hold one of the liquid gelatins while you're building up the layers in your bowl or ring mold.

2. Heat 1 cup of water to boiling and stir in the packet of blueberry gelatin until it has dissolved. Remove from the heat and stir in either 1 cup of the desired juice, or 1 more cup of water; set aside. Now prepare the green gelatin in the same way.

3. Measure 1 cup of the blue gelatin and place it in the bottom of the bowl. If using a ring mold, lightly spritz it with non-stick cooking spray for easier removal. Chill this layer, preferably in the freezer for fastest results, until it is just firm. Carefully place half the grapes on top.

4. Now gently pour 1 cup of the green gelatin over the blue gelatin and grapes, and again chill until firm. Repeat these steps in order with the remaining blue gelatin, grapes, and green gelatin. Once the final layer of green has been poured, be sure to place your bubble bowl or ring into the refrigerator rather than keeping it in the freezer. If the gelatin actually freezes, it will break down and become watery when thawed.

To unmold a bubble ring, briefly submerge the ring mold not quite to the top in hot water, and immediately turn out onto a serving plate.

Garden Fairy Summer Salad in a Tomato

MAKES TWO GENEROUS SERVINGS.

The garden fairies are especially busy during the late summer, when so many vegetables are ripening all at once. At the end of a long, hot day, they recommend a relaxing supper featuring this tasty, colorful salad of tomatoes, corn, beans, and cucumber all picked fresh from the garden. The tomatoes not only form a little bowl, they are also part of the salad! The nasturtium blossoms add a colorful touch, and you can eat them, as well, if you like their peppery taste! (Some fairies love them, some fairies don't). *Hint*: if you have lots of cherry tomatoes, you can substitute a cup or so of them for the larger tomatoes. Cut each in half and toss together with the other ingredients. Serve in salad plates or bowls.

2 medium-sized fresh slicing tomatoes, or
    1 large one
Sea salt, optional
½ cup fresh cooked green beans, cut in
    1-inch slices
½ cup fresh cooked corn, cut from the cob
    (roasted corn is especially good)
¼ cup diced fresh cucumber
Favorite salad dressing, such as French,
    Italian, or ranch
Nasturtium blossoms, optional

1. If you're using two smaller tomatoes, cut a narrow slice from the top of each. Remove any remaining core, along with the seeds and gooey insides. If using one large tomato, cut it into two even sections, so that each half will stand on its own. Scoop out the insides as you would for the smaller tomatoes. Season your tomatoes lightly with a bit of salt, if you wish.

2. Combine the beans, corn, and cucumber in a small bowl. Stir in about 2 tablespoons of your preferred salad dressing. Divide the salad evenly between the tomatoes and garnish with the nasturtium blossoms. Enjoy with crusty bread or rolls and butter for a simple lunch or supper, or as a side dish for a heartier meal.

FERN SOUP

MAKES 4 SERVINGS.

As the winter snows melt and the first spring greens begin to sprout in the warm sun, the fairies keep a sharp eye out for a special type of fern. Although many ferns resemble little fiddleheads when they first begin to unfurl, only one, the Ostrich Fern, can be used for cooking. Since these special ferns are only accessible to the most skilled woodland fairies for a very brief time each spring, their cousins the garden fairies have discovered a wonderful substitute. The asparagus they cultivate not only makes delicious soup, but the mature asparagus stalks actually produce light, airy "ferns" that look lovely in bouquets! And of course, the fairies also use them as a garnish for this creamy "fern" soup.

2 cups thinly sliced asparagus
2 cups vegetable broth
1 cup half-and-half or light cream
2 tablespoons cornstarch or potato starch
⅛ teaspoon grated nutmeg
A few grinds of pepper
A few grinds of sea salt
Asparagus ferns, optional

1. Combine sliced asparagus in a medium saucepan with the vegetable broth. Bring to a boil, reduce the heat, and boil gently for about 5 minutes, until the asparagus is just tender.

2. While this mixture is cooking, combine the half-and-half, cornstarch or potato starch, and nutmeg, whisking it smooth. Whisk this into the cooked vegetable mixture and again bring to a boil. Boil gently for another 2–3 minutes, adding a few grinds of pepper and salt, if you wish. (Different types of broth will have different amounts of seasoning in them.) Serve your Fern Soup while it's nice and hot, garnished on the side, if you wish, with asparagus fern.

Celestial Soup

MAKES 4 SERVINGS.

Have you ever heard of the word "syzygy?" In astronomical terms, it refers to when the earth, sun, and another celestial body, such as a planet or the moon, are all positioned in a straight line with one another. The fairies, always keen on observing the night skies, are especially happy when the earth is aligned in such a manner. They enjoy pretty much anything to do with the moon, stars, sun, and planets—especially dancing by the light of a full summer moon! This fun soup has moons, stars, and planets floating around in it, made from veggies and pasta. Try lining them up to form your own special syzygy, right in your soup bowl!

2½ cups of your favorite broth

⅓ cup thinly sliced carrots; purple carrots will give you a pretty ring in the middle!

⅓ cup thinly sliced yellow summer squash; the smaller in diameter the better, each cut in half

⅓ cup tiny star-shaped pasta (uncooked)

½ cup fresh or frozen peas

¼ teaspoon mixed Italian herbs, optional

Assorted cherry tomatoes (yellow cherry tomatoes can add the sun to your soup), optional

Grated or shredded Parmesan cheese for topping, optional

1. Place the broth and sliced carrots in a medium saucepan; bring to a boil, lower the heat, and simmer, covered, for about 3 minutes. Add the summer squash and pasta. Bring this to a boil once again, stir it well, reduce heat, and simmer for 4 minutes.

2. Add the peas and the herbs, if you are using them. Cook, stirring occasionally, for another 2 minutes, until everything is nicely heated through and the veggies are crisp-tender. Ladle into bowls and add about 3 cherry tomatoes to each, if you wish. Sprinkle with cheese if desired, and serve nice and hot.

Water Sprites' Watermelon Soup

MAKES 4 SERVINGS.

Watermelon is so cool and refreshing on a hot summer day! It is perfect for any fairy gathering, most especially for the garden and water fairies, who are so active during June, July, and August. An occasional adventuresome water sprite has been known to try and dive right into a watermelon bowl full of this soup! Of course, water sprites are much smaller, and evidently also have much less self-control, than most humans. We would surely not want to waste such tasty soup! For variety, try using yellow watermelon in place of the traditional pink or red. Or, make up a batch of each and swirl them in the serving bowls for an especially pretty treat! The amount of sweetener you use in your soup will depend upon the sweetness of the melon, and also your personal preference.

4 cups cubed seedless watermelon
2 tablespoons lime juice
1–2 tablespoons honey or agave nectar
$\frac{1}{16}$ teaspoon (that's a small pinch) of
    sea salt

1. Combine everything in a blender and blend until smooth. Garnish, if you wish, with watermelon lily flowers on top of kiwi fruit lily pads. Water Sprites' Watermelon Soup is especially pretty when served in a hollowed-out watermelon shell. Just be on the lookout for over-active water sprites!

Winter Woods Creamy Vegetable Soup

MAKES 4 SERVINGS.

Northern woodland fairies are especially fond of this when they celebrate the longest night of the year, and other special winter events. It is thought variations of the recipe may have been handed down through their Scandinavian fore-fairies, the Tomten and Nisser. Lots of tasty vegetables combine with the creamy, cheesy base for a flavorful and comforting soup that will warm any fairy up on a cold winter day. The optional topping of purple cauliflower or red cabbage add pretty color and a nice crunch. Buttered toast or some of your favorite crackers make nice accompaniments.

2 cups vegetable broth
1 cup diced red-skinned potato
1 cup frozen mixed vegetables
¼ teaspoon dried dill weed
¼ teaspoon salt
Few grinds black pepper, optional
½ cup diced fresh broccoli
½ cup milk
½ cup cream
2 tablespoons cornstarch or potato starch
2 ounces (½ cup) shredded cheese, such as Colby-Jack
¼ cup diced fresh purple cauliflower or finely shredded red cabbage, optional

1. Combine the broth, potatoes, mixed vegetables, dill weed, salt, and pepper in a medium saucepan. Bring to a boil, then reduce the heat and cook gently for about 5–7 minutes, until the veggies are just tender.

2. Add the broccoli and bring to a boil once again.

3. Combine the milk, cream, and corn or potato starch until smooth. Stir into the soup and again bring just to a boil to thicken. Stir the shredded cheese into the hot soup, stirring until melted, and allow to simmer 2–3 minutes to blend flavors.

4. After ladling out four servings for hungry fairies, top each bowl of hot soup with one tablespoon of the cauliflower or cabbage, if you wish.

To Sip or Spread

The fairies have decided to share just a few of their favorite specialties. Wild Violet Jelly and Crimson Jam are more complex than many of the other recipes, as extra steps must be added to successfully preserve them. It's important that an adult person helps supervise when preparing these recipes, just to be on the safe side. Fortunately, the procedure becomes easier with every batch you make. Once you have made your own jam or jelly and taste how yummy it is, you will want to make more! All the wild violet recipes also require many fresh violets, which around my house can only be gathered in springtime. However, there are also three fairy-favorite beverage recipes, one warm and two cold, that do not use violets and are very easy to make all year round.

Wild Violet Nectar and Syrup

MAKES 2 CUPS OF VIOLET NECTAR.

Harvesting wild violets is an annual spring event for many fairies. They steep the blossoms in hot water to form a bright blue nectar that can then be used to make syrups and jellies. It is extremely important to use only clean, fresh wild violets that have not been exposed to any chemicals, roadside dust, or had dogs or cats wandering around on them. Fortunately, wild violets love to grow in fields and woodlands where such things aren't likely to have happened. I also pick them from my lawn, because I know we never use any chemicals or fertilizers on it. Do not confuse wild violets with "African Violets" that are sold as potted plants! African violets are not edible! For this recipe, use only the violet blossoms; not the stems or leaves. Snap them off with your fingers just at the base of the blossom. Sometimes the fairies will even pull the petals off and only use them, but this can be rather time-consuming! Packing the flowers lightly into a large glass measuring cup is a good way to gauge how many you have picked.

4 cups freshly picked wild violets
2 cups water

1. Place the violets into a heatproof, non-reactive bowl, large measuring cup, or two-quart jar.

2. In a tea kettle or saucepan, bring the water to a boil. Remove it from the heat and pour over the violets, pushing them down into the liquid so that they are all submerged.

3. Cover with a lid or piece of plastic wrap and allow the violets to steep in the water for approximately 24 hours. This is long enough for the water to take up the violet essence without starting to spoil.

4. Pour the liquid through a fine strainer lined with cheesecloth, gently pressing out all the liquid from the violets. Once you've extracted all the liquid, pour it into a pint jar and store, covered, in the refrigerator for up to a week. This makes two cups of violet nectar, ready to be turned into jelly or syrup. Discard the pressed violets; they have already given their color and flavor to the nectar!

To prepare Wild Violet Syrup:

1. Combine equal parts nectar and granulated sugar in a small stainless steel or tempered glass saucepan. Carefully heat, stirring constantly, until the sugar is dissolved. Do not boil the syrup; it could change the color and flavor.

2. Store the syrup in a covered glass jar in the refrigerator for up to two weeks. For longer storage, place in the freezer. This can be done by storing it in covered glass or plastic containers, making sure to leave a little space at the top of each (because the syrup will expand slightly as it freezes). Or, you could pour it into ice cube trays. Once it is frozen solid, remove the syrup cubes and place in labeled freezer bags. It is best when used within a few months.

3. Try mixing with equal parts of sparkling water for an intriguing cold beverage, or add a bit to a cup of hot tea. The fairies often enjoy sipping theirs from dainty cups made of hollowed-out nut shells.

Wild Violet Jelly

MAKES 4 OR 5 QUARTER PINT JELLIES.

It goes without saying that fairies love jelly; especially when it is made from lovely flowers! Making jelly is a grown-up kind of occupation, because you are handling very hot liquids that can spill easily, but it is actually not that difficult, once you understand the steps. The most complicated part is processing the jelly, a step that is important so that there is no chance it might spoil. A canning kettle works best for this. You must be able to fit a metal rack of some sort into the pan, so that the jars of jelly are not in direct contact with the bottom of the pan (they might break from the heat), and it must be deep enough so that you can cover the jars with at least one inch of water over the tops. Aside from this, you will need jelly jars and lids, a pair of specially curved tongs to safely lift the hot jars, and a small funnel and/or heatproof liquid measuring cup for pouring the hot jelly into the jars before processing. This recipe will make about four or five ¼ pint sized jars of jelly. If you have a little extra jelly, don't try processing a partially full jar of it; simply pour it into a heatproof dish such as a custard cup to enjoy once it has cooled. Refrigerate it for up to a month. As an alternative to processing, you can also follow the recipe up to the point where you pour the hot jelly into the jars. Remember to still leave ½ inch of room for expansion at the top of each. Loosely screw on the lids, allow the jars of jelly to cool thoroughly, and then store them in the freezer. Remove one at a time to store in the fridge and enjoy within a month.

1 cup Wild Violet Nectar
2 tablespoons pure lemon juice
1 pouch small-batch powdered pectin
  (0.4-ounce size)
2 cups granulated cane sugar
4 or 5 quarter pint jelly glasses, lids, and
  rims

1. Wash the jelly jars with hot soapy water; rinse well, and place in a pan of hot water. Allow them to simmer, not boil, on the stove while making the jelly. Wash and rinse the lids and rims; set aside in a clean space. If you will be processing the jelly, fill your canning kettle with a few inches of hot water and place over low heat to simmer.

2. Combine the Wild Violet Nectar, lemon juice, and pectin in a deep stainless-steel saucepan and bring to a full boil, stirring with a large, non-reactive spoon. Add the sugar all at once and, stirring well, bring the mixture to a full, rolling boil. This means the liquid will be bubbling all over the surface and will continue to bubble even when you are stirring it. Once it has reached this point, stop stirring and boil it for 1 minute. Turn off the heat and stir again, skimming any foam that may have accumulated on the top.

3. Drain the jelly glasses, placing them on a clean dry surface (I use a fresh dish towel to buffer them). Immediately pour the hot jelly into the glasses, leaving about ½ inch of space at the top of each. Using a funnel will make this much neater and easier. Wipe around the edges of the rims if any of the hot jelly has spilled over them, and carefully place the lids and rims on top, screwing them on to hold in place. The jars of jelly will be *very hot*; use a pot holder, dish towel, or folded paper towel to protect your fingers while screwing the tops on! At this point, you will either allow the jars of jelly to cool and later store them in the freezer, or finish the preserving process as follows.

4. Using jelly making tongs, carefully lower each jar of jelly into the simmering water in the canning pan. Add more of the hot water to cover the jars with at least 1 inch of water above the tallest jar. Cover the pan, increase the heat, and bring to a boil. The jelly needs to be processed for 10 minutes. You can reduce the heat during the boiling process, but it must stay boiling for the entire 10 minutes to safely preserve the jelly.

5. Once the 10 minutes is up, turn off the heat and carefully remove the lid, tilting it away from you so the steam does not burn you. Using the tongs, carefully remove each jar to a flat, padded surface and allow to cool entirely. You will hear the lids make a popping noise as each one seals. Any jars that don't seal should be stored in the refrigerator and used within a month. Enjoy your jelly dabbed on bread or toast, in the middle of a thumbprint cookie, or as a topping for Wild Violet Tea Sandwiches.

CRIMSON BERRY JAM

MAKES SIX ¼ PINT JARS OF JAM.

Fairies love the special days in midsummer when there are still strawberries to be picked, and the raspberries have begun to ripen, also. They scurry around, gathering enough berries to make this special, bright red jam. It doesn't even need to be cooked, which is especially nice during hot weather! You may use small glass jam jars if you prefer, but ½ cup sized snap top plastic containers also work well. This recipe will produce about six ½ cup (¼ pint) sized jars of jam. If you prefer, and have freezer space for lots of containers, you can easily double the ingredients.

2 cups fresh strawberries
2 cups red raspberries
1⅔ cups granulated sugar
½ package (2 tablespoons + 2 teaspoons) reduced-sugar pectin (usually sold in a pink package)

1. Wash and hull the strawberries. Blend or process them on the "chop" setting until they are diced finely but not totally smooth. You can also do this by hand with a pastry cutter, or chop them very fine with a sharp knife.

2. Rinse the raspberries and blend or mash them until they are a bit smoother than the strawberries.

3. Measure out approximately equal portions of the berries to equal 2 cups of fruit in total. (If you have any leftover berries, they can be eaten with cereal, yogurt, ice cream, or just enjoyed plain, with or without a bit of sugar.)

4. In a large saucepan, stir together the sugar and powdered pectin. Add the water and bring to a boil over medium high heat, stirring constantly. Continue to boil, stirring, for 1 minute. Remove from the heat and add the berries, again stirring for 1 minute to thoroughly combine.

5. Pour into clean jars or containers, leaving ½ inch space at the top, and allow to sit, undisturbed, until the jam has cooled to room temperature.

6. Place the tops on the containers and allow the jam to set overnight at room temperature. It is now ready to either refrigerate and eat within a few weeks, or freeze to enjoy later. Do not leave the jam at room temperature for a prolonged period, as the fruit in the jam will spoil if it's left for too long.

RAINBOW FLOATS

MAKES AS MANY FLOATS AS YOU WISH.

What a pretty way to cool down on a hot summer afternoon! These colorful floats will make you think of water fairies peeking up out of a sun-dappled pool to enjoy the rainbow after the storm clouds blow away. Since they can be made with any reasonably clear, light colored juice, numerous flavor combinations are possible. If you're serving Rainbow Floats to several people at once, you may prefer to simply add a few drops of the blue food coloring to a large container of your preferred juice, rather individual glasses as is suggested for a single serving.

Lemonade, limeade, white grape juice, or
   apple juice
Blue food coloring
Sparkling water, flavor of choice
Rainbow sherbet

1. This looks nicest in a tall, clear glass. Fill glass about half full with your juice of choice. Carefully add 1 drop of blue food coloring to the juice in the glass, to tint it a pale shade of blue.

2. Pour in sparkling water to fill the glass ¾ full.

3. Gently float a scoop of rainbow sherbet in your pretty blue juice and serve with a spoon. Note: For a "sunset" rainbow float, substitute raspberry lemonade for the other juices, and omit the blue food coloring.

Sparkling White Hot Chocolate

MAKES 1 SERVING.

This is a wonderful wintertime treat, especially enjoyed by the forest fairies during the short, cold days and long, cold nights of December, January, and February. It is frequently the warm drink of choice at the various fairy winter celebrations. Sparkling White Chocolate really hits the spot after a snowy afternoon spent sledding, skiing, or skating. Adding just a drop of mint extract will give your hot white chocolate a pleasing, minty flavor.

1 cup milk
1 ounce of white chocolate, chopped
1 marshmallow
Sparkling clear sugar
1 drop mint extract, optional

1. Heat the white chocolate in a small, microwave-safe bowl in a microwave oven for about 20–30 seconds at a time, checking carefully to see when it begins to melt. Once it looks about half melted, stir with a spoon until the white chocolate is nice and smooth. Be careful not to overheat the chocolate, as it could actually become hard and difficult to work with.

2. Spread a very small amount of the melted white chocolate on one end of the marshmallow and then dip into the sparkling white sugar; set aside.

3. Carefully smooth a tiny bit of the melted white chocolate around the rim of your mug and sprinkle the rim with a bit of the sparkling sugar, as well. Meanwhile, heat the milk in a small saucepan until it's just steaming but not too hot. Pour a little of the hot milk into the melted chocolate, stirring it well. If you would like to make your white chocolate minty, add one drop of mint extract. Just be careful not to add too much, because mint extract is very strong!

4. Pour this mixture back into the rest of the hot milk, and then carefully pour it into the sugar-rimmed mug. Add in the sparkling marshmallow, and enjoy!

Sunset Fruit Refreshers

MAKES 2 LARGE SERVINGS OR 4 SMALL ONES.

Sunset is a special time for fairies—it's that magical period between daylight and dusk when they are frequently most active. They absolutely love the many colors of a vibrant sunset! Later, as the darkness grows, they may even compete with fireflies to see whose lights are the brightest. Sunset Fruit Refreshers are a cool and flavorful beverage to sip on a warm summer evening, whether you happen to spy any fairies or fireflies, or not.

Usually the fruit and pineapple juice provide enough sweetness on their own. If the strawberries or peaches aren't quite as sweet as you'd prefer, add about a tablespoon of sugar, agave, or honey while the fruit is pureeing.

1 cup fresh strawberries
1 cup fresh, canned, or frozen peaches
1½ cups pineapple juice
Small amount of honey, agave nectar, or
    sugar, optional

1. Wash the strawberries and remove the stems and hulls; set aside. If you are using canned peaches, drain well. If you are using frozen peaches, thaw and drain.

2. To construct the Sunset Fruit Refreshers, place the strawberries and ¼ cup of the pineapple juice in a blender; blend until smooth. Divide evenly between four small clear tumblers or goblets, or two large ones.

3. Next, combine the peaches and another ¼ cup of the pineapple juice in the blender and again blend until smooth. Carefully pour this over the strawberry mixture in each glass. The two layers may combine a bit, but the colors should still remain distinct.

4. Divide the remaining cup of pineapple juice evenly between the glasses. Pouring it gently from a glass measuring cup will help keep the other layers intact. The pineapple juice itself will slowly sink to the bottom, forming the "sunset."

5. Garnish with a fruited skewer and/or fancy straws and enjoy!

FAIRY DESSERT DELIGHTS

Fairies in general consume a very healthy diet. However, there is no question that the average fairy also has a decided sweet tooth. Frequently their desserts feature the fruits, berries, nuts, and honey they are so fond of, but on occasion, wonderful little cakes and tarts are baked. Cupcakes are a special treat, and we have included a few here that will add a fairy-like touch to any event you might choose for serving them.

The Honey-Bee Fairies

Strawberry Fairy Fluff

MAKES ABOUT 6 CUPS.

According to the garden fairies, there is nothing better than sweet, sun-ripened strawberries. I think many of us would agree with them! Strawberry Fairy Fluff combines fresh strawberries with beaten egg white and whipped cream to create fluffy, pink perfection! This recipe utilizes dried egg whites, available in most larger grocery stores. Since these whites have already been pasteurized, there is no question of possible food contamination from using uncooked eggs. They also help stabilize the fluff, which will keep for 2-3 days covered, in the fridge.

2 cups (about ½ pound) washed, hulled strawberries
1 packet unflavored gelatin powder
½ cup + ¼ cup cold water, divided
Tiny pinch of salt
4 teaspoons dried egg whites
½ cup + 2 tablespoons granulated sugar, divided
½ cup heavy cream

1. Puree the strawberries in a blender or food processor until they are smooth and juicy.

2. Soften the gelatin powder in the ½ cup of cold water and stir into the strawberries, along with ¼ cup of the sugar and the tiny pinch of salt. Heat this mixture in a medium saucepan until it just comes to boiling, stirring constantly. This will dissolve the gelatin and make your fairy fluff nice and smooth.

3. Now place the hot saucepan into a larger pan or bowl of ice water, to cool it down quickly. While it is cooling, beat together the dried egg whites and ¼ cup of cold water. Beat at high speed until they form soft peaks. Gradually add in ¼ cup of sugar, about a tablespoon at a time, continuing to beat at high speed until the mixture is thick and

billowy. At this point the strawberry gelatin mixture should have cooled down and started to thicken.

4. Scrape the beaten egg whites into another large bowl and gently fold the thickened strawberries. Whip the heavy cream and remaining 2 tablespoons of sugar until soft peaks form. You can use the mixing bowl and beater without rinsing them, because the cream isn't bothered by a little egg white. If you try to reverse the order, however, the whites will not whip because of the fat in the cream. Be sure not to overbeat the cream, because, unlike the egg whites that can be whipped for a long time, once the cream stiffens it should be used; if overbeaten, it will separate and turn into sweetened butter!

5. Fold the whipped cream gently into the strawberry-egg white mixture and immediately pour into either individual serving bowls or one large bowl. Refrigerate at once; it will continue to thicken slightly while it cools. Garnish with more fresh strawberries or with Fruited Fairy Dust (page 117), with or without a dab of whipped cream.

CREAM PUFF FAIRY RING

MAKES 8-12 SERVINGS.

Fairy rings, also referred to as elf or brownie rings, are said to be formed magically from fairies and their kin dancing about in the moonlight. Actual "fairy rings" are made up of mushrooms growing in a large circle, and there really is a scientific explanation for this. However, I prefer to think of fairies dancing in the moonlight as being more fun. In the olden days, people were afraid to step inside a fairy ring, because they were worried that they would be transported to the fairies' world and never be able to return home! A more practical reason not to step inside one is because, while some mushrooms that form these rings are edible, others are poisonous, and it's not always easy to tell them apart. So, if you're ever lucky enough to discover a fairy ring in a field or forest, it's better just to look and enjoy, rather than tempting the fairies and touching the mushrooms! This fairy ring has no mushrooms in it; it is made from cream puff batter baked in a ring, filled with pudding and whipped cream, and garnished with fruit. There are several tasty combinations suggested. If you wish to make your fairy ring more authentic, feel free to add in some Meringue Mushrooms around the edges. Perhaps you'll even spy a fairy or two, peeking out at you!

½ cup water
¼ cup butter
1 teaspoon sugar
½ teaspoon salt
½ cup bread flour
2 large eggs
1 cup heavy cream
1 package dry instant pudding mix, your choice of flavor
1 cup milk + 2 tablespoons milk, divided
1 cup confectioner's sugar
½ teaspoon vanilla extract
Fresh or dried flowers, fresh fruits or berries, Fruited Fairy Dust (page 117), colorful sprinkles, flaked coconut (either toasted or tinted green), shaved chocolate, toasted sliced almonds (see suggested combinations at the end of the recipe)
Meringue Mushrooms (page 127) for garnishing, optional

1. Preheat oven to 425°; line a baking sheet with parchment paper. Trace around a 9-inch cake pan with a pencil or pen, onto the center of the parchment (do not cut out the circle). This will serve as a guide for piping or spooning the batter in a neat ring. Flip the parchment over so that the cream puff batter will not come into direct contact with the ink or graphite.

2. Combine the water, butter, sugar, and salt in a medium saucepan. Bring to a boil over medium high heat. Stir in the flour all at once, stirring vigorously (a wooden spoon works well for this) until the mixture comes together into a ball.

3. Remove from the heat and beat the eggs in, one at a time. Make sure everything is very well combined; the mixture should look glossy and smooth. Allow it to cool for a couple of minutes, stirring occasionally. This will make it easier to portion out in a circle.

4. Either scoop the mixture into a large pastry bag with a 1-inch tip, or use a spoon to carefully form 8 even mounds of cream puff dough. They should form a circle on the

continued on next page

base you've drawn, with an opening in the middle. Using a spatula, carefully spread the individual cream puffs into one large ring. If the top appears rough, you can dip your fingertips in cool water to smooth it.

5. Bake on a middle rack for 15 minutes at 425°. Reduce the heat to 350°, leaving the pan in the unopened oven, and continue to bake for approximately 25–30 minutes longer. The cream puff ring should be deep golden brown and appear somewhat dry. It should be slightly puffed, but don't worry if it's not terribly high. There should be a little air pocket running around the center of the ring. Carefully piercing the side of the ring with a sharp knife tip in a few places will enable steam to escape, ensuring that your ring stays nice and crisp.

6. Turn the oven off and leave the fairy ring in it, with the door slightly ajar, until it has cooled completely. The ring may now be either filled or frozen for future use. It can also be wrapped and placed flat in the fridge for overnight storage.

7. Just before serving, carefully slice the ring in half horizontally with a large, serrated knife and lift the top off whole.

8. Whip the cream until soft peaks form; set aside. Combine the dry pudding mix and 1 cup milk and beat or whisk for about one minute, until the mixture is well blended. Fold the pudding into the whipped cream and dollop about half of it evenly onto the base of the ring; it should firm up fairly quickly.

9. Add fruit or berries, if you wish, the rest of the pudding mixture, and replace the top. Stir together the confectioner's sugar, 2 tablespoons milk, and vanilla and smooth evenly over the ring. Add any desired decorations and accompaniments, such as fruits not included in the ring. Just before serving, garnish with Meringue Mushrooms, if you desire.

Suggested pudding combinations for the Cream Puff Fairy Ring:

Pistachio pudding mix: Decorate ring with fresh or dried edible flowers and/or colorful sprinkles. Serve with fresh sliced peaches, mangos, or strawberries, either inserted on top of the pudding, or on the side.

Banana Cream pudding mix: Dollop in half the filling; add a layer of sliced bananas and/or mango, and/or strawberries and then the rest of the filling. Top the iced ring with shaved chocolate, and some Fruited Fairy Dust (page 117), if you wish. If not enjoying right away, serve the fruit on the side rather than in the filling.

Chocolate pudding mix: Either layer the filling with pitted sweet cherries, sliced strawberries, and/or red raspberries, or serve them on the side. Garnish the iced top with colorful sprinkles, Fruited Fairy Dust (page 117), edible flowers, and/or chocolate mini chips/shaved chocolate.

Vanilla pudding mix: Layer or serve with blueberries, raspberries, and/or sliced peaches. Garnish the iced ring with edible flowers, toasted coconut, toasted sliced almonds, and/or shaved chocolate.

Lemon pudding mix: Layer or serve with blackberries, blueberries, and/or sliced peaches. Top the iced ring with green tinted coconut and/or colorful sprinkles and/or edible flowers.

Pixies' Pineapple Rice Cream

MAKES 6 SERVINGS.

Although tropical fruits aren't widely used among fairies, the fairies are all incredibly fond of sweet and fruity desserts. *Pixies' Pineapple Rice Cream* has the additional appeal of looking so pretty and colorful, with the multicolored mini marshmallows peeking through the cream. It makes a dessert any pixie would surely love!

8-ounce can crushed pineapple in juice
Water
¼ cup uncooked jasmine rice
1 cup multicolored mini marshmallows
½ cup well-drained mandarin orange
   sections, optional
¾ cup heavy cream
3 tablespoons sugar

1. Drain the pineapple very well, reserving the juice; pressing the pineapple with the back of a spoon while it's in a fine mesh strainer is a good way to ensure this.

2. Measure the pineapple juice and add water to equal 1 cup total. Combine this in a small saucepan with the rice. Bring this to a boil, cover tightly, and reduce the heat to the lowest setting. Simmer the rice for 15 minutes. Turn off the heat but leave the rice, tightly covered, on the burner for another 10 minutes, to complete the absorption of the liquids.

3. Combine the rice with the drained, crushed pineapple. Transfer to a medium sized bowl and cool to room temperature.

4. Gently stir in the mini marshmallows, and the mandarin orange sections, if using. Refrigerate, covered, until the mixture is completely chilled. This is easy to do a day in advance, if you wish.

5. Whip the cream with the sugar until it forms soft peaks. Fold into the pineapple rice mixture. Spoon into serving dishes. If desired, top with a few colorful sprinkles, additional mini marshmallows, or extra pieces of fruit.

Chocolate Cocoa Cupcakes

MAKES 8 CUPCAKES.

Although they dearly love fruits and nuts, most fairies also enjoy a bit of chocolate now and again. Moist, dark Chocolate Cocoa Cupcakes form the base for Fairy Mound Cupcakes (page 99) and Firefly Cupcakes (page 101).

If you prefer, the batter may also be baked in a buttered and floured 6- or 8-inch cake tin. Increase the baking time slightly, depending on the size of the tin and depth of the batter. Cool the cake on a wire rack for 10 minutes before turning it out of the pan (or leave it in if you prefer). After cooling completely, frost as desired.

½ cup cake flour
½ cup sugar
3 tablespoons unsweetened cocoa powder
¼ teaspoon baking soda
¼ teaspoon baking powder
¼ teaspoon salt
3 tablespoons corn oil
½ teaspoon vanilla extract
1 large egg
⅓ cup water
¼ cup chocolate mini chips, optional

1. Preheat oven to 350°. Prepare cupcake tin by lining with eight non-stick cupcake liners or by spraying each with non-stick cooking spray and lightly dusting with flour.

2. Combine all the dry ingredients in a medium mixing bowl.

3. Whisk in the oil, vanilla, egg, water, and mini chips, if desired, until the batter is smooth.

4. Divide evenly between the eight liners and bake for about 20 minutes, until puffed and firm to touch. Cool in the tin for 5–10 minutes before carefully loosening them and turning out to cool completely on a wire rack.

Fairy Mound Cupcakes

MAKES 8 CUPCAKES.

Fairy mounds are thought to have been the ancient homes of Scottish and Irish fairies' long-ago ancestors. Some of the best-known fairy mounds can still be seen today on the Isle of Skye, off the coast of Scotland. While these ancient mounds are covered simply with grass, or occasionally trees, modern-day fairies think they'd be much prettier fancied up with flowers blooming on them. In an unusual twist, chocolate cupcakes are frosted upside-down with thick, fluffy frosting and topped with grass-green coconut and whatever pretty decorations you wish, to form tempting, miniature fairy mounds. Using dried egg whites rather than fresh means there is no need to cook the frosting, and also helps to give it a thick, creamy texture.

Chocolate Cocoa Cupcakes batter (page 97)
(Add mini chocolate chips, if you wish)

Coconut Grass
12 drops green food coloring
6 drops yellow food coloring
2 teaspoons water
1½ cups flaked coconut

Fluffy White Frosting
1 tablespoon + 1 teaspoon dried egg white
¼ cup water
1 teaspoon vanilla extract
⅛ teaspoon salt
½ cup fine granulated sugar
Optional: Fresh or dried edible flowers,
Fondant Flowers (page 119), and/or
colorful sprinkles

1. Prepare the cupcake batter as directed, spraying or buttering the cupcake tins and dusting with flour rather than using liners. Bake the 8 cupcakes for the time listed. Once they are baked, allow them to cool in the tins for about 10 minutes. Then carefully loosen around the edges and remove them, turning each cupcake upside down to complete cooling on a wire rack.

2. While the cupcakes are either baking or cooling, color the flaked coconut by combining the green and yellow food coloring and the water in a medium sized bowl. Add in the coconut and stir it around very well, until the flakes are all evenly colored. Spread on a baking sheet to dry.

3. To make the frosting, combine the powdered egg white, water, vanilla, and salt in a medium mixing bowl. Beat on low speed with the whisk attachment until the egg whites have absorbed the water and are foamy, scraping the bowl occasionally as needed. Increase speed to medium-high and continue beating the whites until they begin to hold their shape.

4. Add the sugar gradually, about a tablespoon at a time, continuously beating, until stiff, glossy peaks form. Your frosting is now ready to use!

5. To construct the Fairy Mounds, spread each upside-down cupcake with a generous coating of the frosting and sprinkle with the grass-green coconut. Garnish with fresh, dried, or fondant flowers or sprinkles as desired. Refrigerate any leftover Fairy Mounds for another day or two.

FIREFLY CUPCAKES

MAKES 8 CUPCAKES.

Imagine frolicsome fairies darting around the early summer meadows and woodlands, playing hide-and-go-seek with the fireflies! So many tiny twinkling lights, all dancing back and forth at once! Each of these luxuriant buttercream and ganache topped chocolate cupcakes has its own sparkling firefly shimmering on the top. You can almost feel the soft breezes blowing on a warm summer night!

Chocolate Cocoa Cupcakes (page 97)
Marshmallow Buttercream (page 102),
   colored firefly yellow (add ½ teaspoon
   orange flavoring, optional)

Chocolate Ganache Glaze
½ cup semi-sweet chocolate chips
2 tablespoons cream
2 teaspoons light corn syrup
Fondant Fireflies (page 123)
Edible golden glitter or sparkly
   yellow sugar

1. Prepare the cupcakes as directed, using cupcake wrappers in the tins. Once they have cooled completely, frost them evenly with the yellow tinted buttercream, saving out a tiny amount for adhering the fireflies, if you wish.

2. Use a flat cake spatula or knife blade, dipped in hot water and wiped dry, to smooth each cupcake's surface as flat as possible. Now place them in the fridge, or briefly in the freezer, to cool and firm the buttercream.

3. While the cupcakes are chilling, combine the chocolate chips, cream, and corn syrup in a microwave-safe container or small saucepan. Microwave for 30 seconds at a time, stirring after each, until the chips are mostly melted; continue to stir until the mixture is smooth and liquid. If using a saucepan, gently heat over low, stirring constantly, until the chocolate is almost all melted. Remove from heat and continue to stir until the mixture is smooth and liquid.

4. Carefully pour the ganache glaze over each chilled cupcake, smoothing it evenly. At this point, place a firefly on each cupcake, sprinkling a bit of glitter or sparkly sugar near its glowing light. Store the cupcakes in the refrigerator until you're ready to enjoy them.

Marshmallow Buttercream

MAKES ENOUGH FROSTING FOR 8 CUPCAKES.

Marshmallow Buttercream has a texture and taste very similar to some of the classic, cooked buttercream frostings, but is much easier to make. It is versatile and can be used either as a frosting or a filling. A variety of flavorings and colors can be added to make each batch unique. This makes enough frosting to generously swirl over each cupcake you're creating, whether Yellow Butter Cupcakes or Chocolate Cocoa Cupcakes. The fairies would definitely approve!

¾ cup butter, softened
1 cup Marshmallow Fluff or crème
½ teaspoon vanilla extract
Desired additional flavorings and colorings
2 cups confectioner's sugar

1. Place the butter in a medium mixing bowl and beat until light and fluffy. Add the marshmallow fluff, vanilla, and any other desired flavorings, again beating until light and fluffy.

2. On low speed, gradually beat in the confectioner's sugar. Add any desired coloring. Increase speed to high and beat until the frosting is smooth and creamy. It is now ready to frost your cupcakes.

Yellow Butter Cupcakes

MAKES 8 CUPCAKES.

These light and buttery little cupcakes are perfect fairy food. This recipe makes 8 good-sized cupcakes; just right for Blue Sky Butterfly Cupcakes (page 105) or Rose Petal Cupcakes (page 107).

    The batter can alternatively be baked in a buttered and floured 6- or 8-inch round cake pan. Add a bit more baking time if using one of the pans rather than cupcake tins. Cool in the pan on a wire rack, removing the cake after 10 minutes (or leave it in the pan, if you prefer), and frost as desired, once fully cooled.

¾ cup cake flour
¼ teaspoon salt
½ teaspoon baking powder
½ cup sugar
¼ cup butter, softened
¼ cup milk
2 teaspoons rose water or ½ teaspoon
    vanilla extract
1 large egg

1. Preheat oven to 350°. Line 8 muffin cups with cupcake liners.

2. Combine the flour, salt, baking powder, and sugar in a medium mixing bowl.

3. Add the soft butter, milk, and rose water. Beat until smooth and creamy.

4. Add the egg and beat again until the batter is nice and smooth; don't overbeat, in order to keep the cupcakes tender. Divide evenly between the cupcake liners. Bake for about 20 minutes, until the cupcakes are light golden brown and spring back when lightly touched.

5. Cool in pans about 5 minutes, and then carefully remove the cupcakes and place on a wire rack to complete cooling.

Blue Sky Butterfly Cupcakes

MAKES BUTTERFLIES FOR 8 CUPCAKES.

What could be better fun for fairies than cavorting with butterflies over a flower-filled meadow on a sunny summer day? These colorful cupcakes feature pretty butterflies made from pretzels and fondant, "flying" through a sky of blue Marshmallow Buttercream. What a yummy way to spend the day!

   These butterflies may either be created the same day you make the cupcakes, or up to a few days in advance.

Yellow Butter Cupcakes (page 103),
   flavored with vanilla extract
Marshmallow Buttercream (page 102),
   colored sky blue (add ½ teaspoon pure
   lemon flavoring, optional)

Pretzel Butterflies
16 white confection (yogurt) dipped
   pretzels
3–4 ounces white chocolate or white
   chocolate chips
Fancy colored sprinkles, in a variety of
   sizes and colors
Mini Marshmallow Fairy Fondant (page
   118), in various colors

1. For the wings, place the pretzels on a waxed paper or parchment lined baking sheet. Break the white chocolate into small pieces and place it or the white chips into a small microwave-safe bowl. Heat for about 30 seconds at a time, stirring in between each heating session.

2. Once the white chocolate or chips are about ⅔ melted, stir until the mixture is smooth and pourable. Using a small spoon, distribute the melted chocolate evenly into all the circular openings in each of the pretzels.

3. Place colorful sprinkles into the melted chocolate, making matching "pairs" to form 8 sets of butterfly wings. Allow the wings to cool thoroughly before constructing the butterflies.

4. For the butterfly bodies, pinch off small pieces of pastel colored Mini Marshmallow Fairy Fondant (page 118), about a teaspoon or less per butterfly. Form each butterfly's body into a long, thin cylinder, with a tapered tail at one end and a slightly round head at the other. If you wish, use a toothpick or fork tine to make two small indents in each butterfly head. Dab with a bit of water and place a tiny sprinkle in each indent for eyes.

5. Either use right away or store with the wings in a cool, dry place on the parchment- or waxed paper-lined baking sheet. Shortly before serving, frost the cooled cupcakes with generous swirls of the blue buttercream.

6. Place a fondant butterfly body in the center of each frosted cupcake. Position two matching wings on either side of the butterfly body, anchoring them in the frosting. If you wish, add some colorful "flower" sprinkles to the frosting. Enjoy your butterfly cupcakes!

Rose Petal Cupcakes

MAKES FROSTING AND PETALS FOR 8 CUPCAKES.

Flower fairies and dairy fairies alike rejoice in Rose Petal Cupcakes! These unique little cakes use rose water to flavor and perfume the cupcakes and cream topping. Red berry jam adds a layer of tart sweetness, and delicate Sugared Rose Petals drift over all. Enjoy these elegant treats with your best fairy china tea set.

Note: It is a good idea to make the Sugared Rose Petals a day or two in advance so that they can fully dry. Try to make them on a sunny day rather than a rainy one.

Yellow Butter Cupcakes (page 103), flavored with rose water
Crimson Berry Jam (page 79) or favorite red berry jam

Whipped Cream Frosting
2 tablespoons cold water
1 teaspoon plain unflavored gelatin powder
1 cup heavy cream, cold
½ cup confectioner's sugar
2 teaspoons rose water or 1 teaspoon pure vanilla extract

Sugared Rose Petals
Fresh rose petals
1 teaspoon dried egg white
1 tablespoon water
Superfine sugar

1. Prepare and cool the cupcakes. To make the whipped cream frosting, place the cold water in a small, microwavable container such as a custard cup. Add the gelatin powder and allow it to soften for a minute. Next, microwave the mixture for about 20–30 seconds, until the gelatin is just dissolved without the water becoming too hot. Allow to cool to room temperature, watching closely as it will begin to harden rapidly.

2. Combine the gelatin with the cold cream, confectioner's sugar, and the rose water or vanilla, stirring to integrate them together. Whip or whisk until the cream forms fairly stiff peaks. You want it firm enough to frost the cupcakes without sliding off, but not so stiff that it begins to separate. If that happens, you will end up with a bowl of sweetened butter instead of whipped cream frosting!

3. Place the whipped cream frosting into a frosting bag with a ½-inch wide tip, plain or serrated. It can be used right away or stored in the refrigerator with the tip covered for up to a couple of days.

4. Spread the cooled cupcakes evenly with a thin layer of the jam. Pipe the frosting generously in swirls onto each cupcake. (You may have a little extra, which can be used in any way you like to enjoy whipped cream.) Just before serving, sprinkle with a few Sugared Rose Petals (directions below). Store the cupcakes in the refrigerator and plan to eat them within a couple of days.

5. To make Sugared Rose Petals: Stir together the egg white and water with a fork, until they are well combined and slightly frothy.

6. Using a small, food-grade brush or your fingertips, gently cover each petal with the egg white mixture. Shake off excess and then dip in or sprinkle with superfine sugar.

7. Place on parchment- or waxed paper-lined baking sheets and allow them to dry completely, which could take from several hours to overnight. Store the dried petals in an airtight container and they will last for several days.

Fairy Berry Tarts

MAKES SIX 4-INCH TARTS.

Sun-drenched berries, plump and sweet, are hand-picked by the woodland fairies every summer. Some are enjoyed by the hungry fairies as soon as they pick them, while others are made into jams and jellies. For a special treat, the very best berries are set aside for one of the fairies' favorite summer desserts, Fairy Berry Tarts. The ruby red raspberry glaze gives the berries in the tarts a jewel-like glow. A little dollop of whipped cream crowning each tart complements the tangy sweet berries perfectly.

Tart Crust
1 cup all-purpose flour
¼ cup packed brown sugar
½ cup butter, slightly softened
1 egg, separated

Berry Filling
¾ cup water, divided
3 cups fresh mixed berries: small whole
    strawberries, blueberries, red and black
    raspberries, blackberries, etc.
1 cup fresh or frozen red raspberries
½ cup granulated sugar
1 tablespoon cornstarch
½ packet unflavored gelatin powder
    (1¼ teaspoons)
Sweetened whipped cream, if you wish

1. To make the crust: Move your oven rack to an upper position and preheat oven to 375°.

2. Combine the flour and brown sugar in a fairly large bowl, stirring it around to mix well.

3. Separate the egg yolk from the egg white; set the white aside in a small bowl.

4. Add the butter, cut in cubes, and the egg yolk, to the sugar and flour. Using your fingers, work them in until everything is well combined and you no longer see either egg yolk or butter; the dough will now stick together.

5. Divide the dough into 6 sections and gently roll each one out a little larger than the diameter of the 4-inch tart tins. Fit into the tins, forming a little mini rim around the edge of each. Place the pastry-lined tart tins on a baking sheet. Chill for about 5 minutes in the freezer or 10–15 minutes in the fridge before baking for best results.

6. Brush the lightly beaten egg white gently over the chilled pastry. Bake for about 20–25 minutes, until the tart shells are golden brown. Allow them to cool thoroughly before filling.

7. To make the Berry Filling: Blend ½ cup of the water and the cup of raspberries until smooth. Strain this liquid to remove the raspberry seeds.

8. Sprinkle the gelatin powder on the remaining ¼ cup of cold water to soften; set aside. Combine the blended raspberry mixture with the cornstarch and sugar in a small saucepan. Bring to a boil over medium heat, stirring constantly to prevent sticking. Stir in the softened gelatin until it is totally dissolved and the mixture is smooth. Remove from the heat and place the pan in a bowl of cold water or ice water to chill quickly. Complete the chilling process in the fridge, if need be.

9. Once the raspberry glaze has thickened somewhat, but can still be easily poured, it is time to assemble your tarts. If possible, place the tins on a platter or cake tin that will fit in your refrigerator. Spoon a bit of the glaze in the bottom of each of the cooled, pastry lined tart tins. Arrange the berries attractively in the tins, mounding them up so that there are plenty of berries in each.

10. Carefully drizzle the glaze evenly over the mounded berries, so that they are glazed evenly and the liquid is about even with the top of the pastry in each tin. Slide the tarts into the refrigerator to chill completely and set the glaze; at least 2 hours, or up to overnight.

11. Serve the tarts right in the tins. Topping with a bit of sweetened whipped cream just before enjoying your Fairy Berry Tarts makes them even more delicious!

Orchard Harvest Apple Tarts

MAKES SIX 4-INCH TARTS.

Harvesting apples is a real adventure for the fairies. The larger apple varieties may necessitate the fairies calling on some of their animal friends to help haul such a bounteous crop home. Squirrels are in high demand for this task due to their climbing agility, but can be a bit too energetic for the fairies to control. Moles are more amenable, but due to their underground habitat unfortunately tend to become disoriented in the bright light of day. Rabbits, large and powerful, can lead the fairies on a high-spirited apple picking adventure! In the end, many fairies prefer their good friends the quiet little chipmunks to help out with both fruit and nut harvests; always making sure there is plenty for the chipmunks, too! Here is a perfect autumn tart, using fresh-from-the-orchard apples and a bit of tasty jam. When making Orchard Harvest Apple Tarts, the filling and crust bake at the same time. They make tarts so delectable, no fairy (or chipmunk!) could resist them.

Almond Tart Crust
¾ cup all-purpose flour
¼ cup almond flour
1 tablespoon sugar
¼ cup cold butter
2 tablespoons cold water

Apple Filling
2–3 smallish baking apples
¼ cup Crimson Berry Jam (page 79) or other favorite jam or preserve such as peach, apricot, raspberry, blackberry
6 tablespoons sugar
½ teaspoon cinnamon
Sweetened whipped cream, if you wish

1. Combine the all-purpose flour, the almond flour, and 1 tablespoon of sugar in a medium-sized bowl, food processor, or blender.

2. Now you may either shred the butter into the dry ingredients, or blend or process the butter and dry ingredients together until it resembles fairly fine crumbs. Add the cold water, mixing just until it is well blended.

3. Divide the dough into 6 even portions and form each into a small ball. Roll out gently on a lightly floured surface to a size slightly larger than each tart tin. Fit the crust into the tins, turning under and pinching the loose edges to form a little rim. Space the tart tins evenly on a baking sheet, but do not bake them yet.

4. Preheat the oven to 375° while filling the unbaked tart shells. Place 2 teaspoons of your preferred jam or preserve in the bottom of each lined tart tin, gently smoothing it to coat the bottom evenly.

5. Peel and thinly slice the apples. Rather than cutting long slices from the entire length of the apple, try cutting shorter slices at a slight angle, as the smaller size fits into the tart tins more easily. Arrange the apple slices decoratively in each tart shell, fitting them as close together as possible. Starting at the outer edge to form a circle and then working your way in toward the center makes a pretty design. You can also place longer slices of apple in a straight line across the center of each tart and then fill in on the edges with shorter slices.

6. Once you have completely filled each tart with apples, combine the cinnamon and sugar in a small bowl. Sprinkle about 1 tablespoon of the mixture evenly over each tart. Slide the baking sheet into the preheated oven and bake for approximately 40 minutes. The apples will bubble up some, as juices are released.

7. When the slices are just barely beginning to brown, it is time to take your tarts out of the oven. Allow them to cool slightly before serving; they are good either at room temperature or chilled. If you like, garnish the center of each tart with a blackberry or raspberry and serve your tarts with lightly sweetened whipped cream.

Fairy Fancies
& Special
Confections

Here are some of those special recipes that make fairy cooking so much fun! Edible fairy dust is sprinkled generously on many different fairy foods, while fondant flowers and insects call to mind flower-filled meadows and sun-dappled forests. Sweet meringue mush-rooms and acorns are a forest friendly delight. A few of the fairies' more unusual treats are also included, such as pretty, edible dessert bowls and chocolatey, fruity frozen ice cream cones. Last but not least is the tasty and colorful fairy favorite, Pixies' Popcorn! The fairies hope you enjoy all their favorite foods.

Fruited Fairy Dust

MAKES AS MUCH FAIRY DUST AS YOU WISH.

Although fairies dearly love fruits and berries, it hasn't always been particularly easy to make them into fairy dust. However, now that packets of freeze-dried fruits can be easily purchased, Fruited Fairy Dust is as easy as the wave of a fairy wand to make. All you need is three or more types of colorful freeze-dried fruits and berries, and either a blender, food processor, or, in a pinch, a good rolling pin. Just be sure that the fruit you are purchasing is *freeze*-dried, which is light and crispy-crunchy, not regular dried, which is usually quite chewy and not at all suited for making proper fairy dust.

Freeze-dried strawberries or raspberries
Freeze-dried mango or peaches
Freeze-dried blueberries

1. Measure out, one at a time, an equal amount of each fruit listed. Depending on how much fairy dust you would like, you could try starting with ½ cup each, which should make a fairly generous sprinkling.

2. In order to keep your dust colorful, it's important to keep the various types of fruit separate from one another. One at a time, blend or process the fruits or berries until they are a combination of fine powder and slightly larger pieces. Empty the fruit into a small, sealable container, scraping or wiping out the blender or processor thoroughly before adding the next fruit. Because the fine powder can be rather sticky, you may prefer to wash the appliance in between each type of fruit; just dry it completely, or the fruit will turn to sticky mush!

3. Repeat the process with the other types of fruits, placing each batch of "dust" into a separate, airtight container. You may also place each batch of powdered fruit into small, zip-lock type plastic bags. If you need to make your fairy dust using a rolling pin, place each type of fruit into separate plastic bags and crush them to the desired consistency with the rolling pin, then store them as above.

4. Keeping the fruit colors separate until it's time to sprinkle them over your favorite food choice will make for prettier, more colorful dust. Simply sprinkle as much as you'd like over the top, and enjoy! It is important to sprinkle Fruited Fairy Dust just before you wish to eat it; otherwise, it may lose its crispy crunch. Plan to use your fairy dust fairly quickly; even in airtight containers, it can turn sticky in damp or humid weather.

Mini Marshmallow Fairy Fondant

MAKES ABOUT 1½ CUPS OF FONDANT.

Fairies are very fond of fondant. Try saying that three times quickly! Mini Marshmallow Fairy Fondant is easy to make and can be stored in the fridge for several weeks. The fairies like to produce several different colors at a time. They can then create all sorts of colorful little decorations from the fondant. You will discover directions for several different treats following this recipe. You will also use it when creating the butterflies for Blue Sky Butterfly Cupcakes (page 105); directions are included in that recipe. The fondant will become firm when it chills in the refrigerator, but becomes soft and malleable again once you begin warming it with your hands.

1 cup mini marshmallows
2 teaspoons water
1¼ cups confectioner's sugar
2½ teaspoons butter
2–4 drops food coloring, optional

1. Combine the mini marshmallows and water in a small- to medium-sized microwave-safe bowl. Microwave for 30 seconds. The marshmallows should look soft and puffy.

2. Stir the mixture with a spoon until all the marshmallows are melted. They should all melt within about half a minute; if a few stubbornly refuse to, you can microwave them for just a few more seconds; try about 10. You do not want to overheat them.

3. If you are using white marshmallows and wish to color them, add 2–4 drops of your desired color. To make a blended color, use two drops of two primary colors, such as red and blue to make pale purple or red and yellow to make light orange. Blue and yellow will produce green, but chances are you already have a little container of green coloring, anyway.

4. Once the marshmallows are nice and smooth, carefully stir in 1 cup of the confectioner's sugar.

It may look a little lumpy; that's okay as long as the lumps are not hardened sugar. If there is a tiny bit of sugar still not fully mixed in, that's okay, too.

5. Using about 2 teaspoons of the butter, smear it evenly in a 12-inch circle on a clean, flat, cool surface. Scrape all the melted marshmallow out onto the buttery circle, and use the remaining butter to coat your fingers well. Gently knead the mixture, pushing it around with your fingertips or buttered hands, until it is smooth and most of the butter has been incorporated.

6. Next, sprinkle the remaining ¼ cup of confectioner's sugar over the fondant. This is what will now keep your fingers from sticking. Gently knead it in until the fondant is mostly not sticky, but still a little soft. It will have a consistency we refer to as "pliable."

7. Carefully place in either a small, tightly lidded container or a sealable sandwich bag. Place in the refrigerator; it will firm up quite a bit when cold. Remove bits of it as needed, to form into whatever amazing shapes you desire; store the rest, tightly sealed, in the refrigerator for up to several weeks.

Fondant Flowers

The fairies love dainty flowers, although they are not averse to napping in a large rose blossom or day lily. Here are simple directions to make tiny flowers such as violets and forget-me-nots, slightly larger flowers such as daisies, and everyone's favorite, roses. Using a set of measuring spoons makes forming symmetrical flowers more precise, although the flowers may be a bit bigger than if you simply pinch off tiny bits of the fondant. Once you have completed each flower, place it on a waxed paper- or parchment-lined baking sheet to dry.

Mini Marshmallow Fairy Fondant (page 118)
Cornstarch
Water
Round colored sprinkles, optional
Additional food coloring, optional

1. For violets, pansies or forget-me-nots: If you choose to measure the fondant, using the smallest size spoon you have will work best, ⅛ of a teaspoon if you have it. You can also pinch off teeny-tiny pieces, especially for the forget-me-nots, which are usually quite delicate. Remember that the fondant will be firm if you've stored it in the fridge, but will soften as you work with it.

2. Roll five evenly sized pieces of your preferred color (blue for forget-me-nots, purple for violets, purple, yellow, and/or orange for pansies) into round balls, and then use your thumb to push each one into a circle. A tiny bit of cornstarch will help keep the fondant from sticking to your fingers or work surface.

3. Now form the "petals" into a flower shape and use a tiny bit of water to attach the petals to one another at the center of the flower. Roll a tiny bit of yellow fondant into a ball for the center of the flower, or use a round sprinkle. Dab a bit of water in the center of the flower to secure the fondant ball or sprinkle. If you wish to add a few

color accents, dilute a drop or two of food coloring in a teaspoon of water.

4. Using a food-safe tiny paintbrush, a toothpick, or your fingertip, gently add colorful accents on the outer edges of each petal. Be careful not to get your flower too wet or the food coloring will run over the surface.

5. If you wish, add a couple of green fondant leaves. To form the leaves, pinch small amounts of the green fondant and roll into balls or oblong shapes. Pinch one end to form the leaf tip and flatten. Add leaf-like accents with a toothpick or knife tip, if you wish. Attach to the flower with a bit of water. Transfer to the lined baking sheet and allow the flower to dry thoroughly at room temperature.

6. For daisies, asters, or zinnias: Use many tiny pieces of your preferred fondant colors; white for daisies, blue, pink, or purple for asters, yellow, pink, or orange for zinnias. Roll each tiny piece into a long thin petal, pinching the ends to points.

7. Dampen one end of each petal, fastening them one to another to form a circle with the inner points connected to one another and the outer points facing out. Attach a small round of yellow fondant to the center of each daisy, or a tiny round of green fondant or a round sprinkle to the center of each aster or zinnia.

8. For roses: Use pink, yellow, orange, white, or purple fondant. Using slightly larger amounts than for the previous flowers, form two or three (or more) small balls of the same color.

9. On a flat surface sprinkled with cornstarch to prevent sticking, roll each ball into a very thin circle and place them end-to-end in a vertical row. Using a Q-tip or very small spoon, moisten a thin line intersecting the middle of each circle, from one edge to the other.

10. Now, starting at the lower/lowest circle, roll it up tightly along the damp center line, leaving the edges loose. Continue to roll the first circle over onto the second one, and then on to the third, so that you have a small, rolled center with "petal" edges on either side.

11. Cut the center to form two halves; each will look like a rosebud or a rose, depending on how many circles you have rolled together. Add a green leaf or two, fastening around the base of each rose, if you wish, and trim any excess from the base. Gently fluff the rose petals out to form your flower.

Fondant Fireflies, Honeybees, and Bumblebees

The fairies find all these insects very useful. They often befriend the hardworking bees, guiding them to the sweetest blooms in the meadows in exchange for a bit of golden honey. In the cool dusk of an early summer evening, spirited games of hide-and-seek are frequently played between fairies and fireflies. And on more than one occasion, a helpful firefly has been known to guide young fairies who have flown too far astray back to their homes, when their fairy lights have dimmed down too much for them to find their way independently. Little fondant honeybees and bumblebees add a decorative touch to many sweet dishes. And fondant fireflies even light up their very own Firefly Cupcakes (page 101)!

Mini Marshmallow Fairy Fondant (page 118), yellow and/or orange
Sliced almonds
Teeny-tiny round sprinkles
Additional food coloring, as needed
Dark cocoa powder, as needed
Sparkling yellow sugar, as needed

1. For Fireflies: Use yellow fondant; pinch a tiny piece and form it into an elongated shape about 1 inch long, with a little rounded head at one end and a tapered tail at the other.

2. Lightly brush with a tiny bit of water. Roll the head and front half of the body in dark cocoa powder, being careful not to get any on the "tail." If you would like the tail brighter, lightly paint it with little diluted yellow food coloring; just don't get it too wet!

3. Using clean fingers, dip the firefly's tail into sparkling yellow sugar. Using a toothpick or tine of a fork, make two tiny indents in the head and insert two tiny round sprinkles for eyes.

4. Gently position two sliced almonds along the firefly's back for wings, smaller ends pointing towards the tail. Insert the rounded ends gently into the firefly's body just to hold them in place, but so that they are still laying mostly flat along the firefly's back.

5. For Honeybees and Bumblebees: There are lots of variations to the various types of bees, so you really can't go wrong when creating one. Mixing half yellow and half orange fondant gives a nice color for most bees.

6. Form a tiny bit into a bumblebee-ish or honey bee-ish shape, about an inch long. Now decide which parts of your bee you'd prefer to be darker and which will remain yellowish-orange.

7. Use the tines of a fork, dipped in dark cocoa powder, to form stripes on the bee. Lightly moisten either the front or back of the bee's body and cover with cocoa powder if you would like it partially dark and partially light.

8. Make two tiny indents in the bee's head and insert a tiny round sprinkle in each for eyes. Use two sliced almonds for wings; insert the narrow end into the bee's body, with the rounded ends sticking out at an angle so that it looks like it's flying along.

Nutty Meringue Acorns

MAKES ABOUT 36 MERINGUE ACORNS.

Each autumn, oak trees in the fairy forests produce a crop of small, capped nuts called acorns. While some harvest years are more bountiful than others, the woodland fairies are generally kept quite busy harvesting, shelling, and then leaching the acorns. Leaching is a process the fairies (and a few people) use to remove the tannins that make most acorns bitter and inedible. The shelled nuts are submerged in cold water for several days in a row, with the tannin-containing water poured off and fresh water added each day, until finally the acorn nut meats lose their bitter taste. This is quite a lot of work, and although the fairies then dry the acorns and grind them into fine meal they use for cooking, most humans simply don't find this at all worth the effort. Fortunately, it's possible to create acorn look-alikes out of meringue. Ground hazelnuts are folded into the stiff, sweet egg white mixture just before the meringues are shaped and slowly dried in a barely warm oven. Adding a little cap of melted chocolate topped with more ground hazelnuts to each meringue makes these tiny sweets look very acorn-like indeed!

2 egg whites, at room temperature
1 teaspoon lemon juice or ⅛ teaspoon
    cream of tartar
⅛ teaspoon salt
½ teaspoon pure vanilla extract
½ cup fine granulated sugar
1 cup ground roasted hazelnuts, divided
½ cup semi-sweet or milk chocolate chips
1 teaspoon coconut oil
1 tablespoon chocolate hazelnut spread

1. Adjust oven racks to the middle position and preheat the oven to 200°.

2. Place the egg whites in a large mixing bowl.

3. Add the lemon juice or cream of tartar, salt, and vanilla. Beat at medium speed until the mixture is foamy. Increase the speed to medium high. Slowly, about a tablespoon at a time, add the sugar. Continue beating until the mixture forms stiff, glossy peaks. It's especially important to have the meringue stiff and stable before adding any nuts, as the oil in them could cause the mixture to deflate otherwise.

4. Gently fold ¼ cup of the ground roasted hazelnuts into the meringue, until just well blended. Spoon into a large pastry bag with a ½ inch wide plain tip. Press out onto parchment lined baking sheets, making the base just slightly larger than the top. Push down and then release slightly to delineate between the "cap" and the "nut." Each acorn should be about an inch wide at the base and 1–1½ inches high, with a cap-like base and slightly pointed tip. Bake for about 2½–3 hours, until they feel dry to touch and lift off the parchment paper, but still have very little color.

5. Cool in the oven for at least another hour, or even up to overnight, before removing. When the meringue acorns are fully cool and dry, melt together the chocolate chips, coconut oil, and chocolate hazelnut spread. This is easiest to do using a small microwave-safe bowl, heating them for 30 seconds at a time until they are melted enough to stir smooth.

6. Dip or smooth the chocolate on the "cap" end of each meringue and then dip into the remaining ground roasted hazelnuts. Place on parchment paper lined trays to cool and set the chocolate.

7. Once the chocolate has hardened, store in an airtight container at room temperature. If kept away from heat and high humidity, they should store well for several days.

Meringue Hints from the Fairies

You will notice this recipe and the next start with the same five basic ingredients; and, especially if you're making the acorns, a full recipe makes quite a few. If you prefer, measure out the meringue after it has been beaten to stiff, glossy peaks, but before you have added the hazelnuts. Use ½ of this to form 12 mushroom caps and stems. Fold 2 tablespoons of ground hazelnuts into the remaining meringue base and use to form approximately 18 acorns. When cooled, put together using ½ the amounts of melted chocolate (and ground hazelnuts) listed in the individual recipes.

MERINGUE MUSHROOMS

MAKES ABOUT 24 MERINGUE MUSHROOMS.

Deep in the forest, multiple mushrooms spring into sight from the middle of summer to the middle of fall. Woodland fairies busily harvest the tastiest of these, always careful to pick edible mushrooms only. The fairies either cook their mushrooms fresh, or dry them to enjoy throughout the coming year. However, there is another type of mushroom much loved of fairies; those made from airy, egg white based meringue. Light and crispy, they melt in your mouth! The fairies also use meringue mushrooms to decorate cake rolls and roulades, especially the fancy holiday cake roll often referred to as a Yule Log or "Bûche de Noël."

2 egg whites, at room temperature
1 teaspoon lemon juice or ⅛ teaspoon
   cream of tartar
½ teaspoon pure vanilla extract
⅛ teaspoon salt
½ cup fine granulated sugar
Unsweetened cocoa powder
½ cup semi–sweet chocolate chips
1 teaspoon coconut oil

1. Preheat the oven to 200°, adjusting racks to middle position. Place the egg whites in a large mixing bowl.

2. Add the lemon juice or cream of tartar, vanilla, and salt. Beat at medium speed until the mixture is foamy. Increase the speed to medium high. Slowly, about a tablespoon at a time, add the sugar. Continue beating until the mixture forms stiff, glossy peaks.

3. Spoon into a large pastry bag with a ½-inch wide plain tip. Using slightly different pressure for caps and stems, squeeze the meringue onto parchment-lined baking sheets. The caps will be flatter and rounder, the stems thinner and taller. Making a row of stems next to each row of caps (the same amount in each) will help ensure that you end up with a matching number of complete

mushrooms. If the caps have a little point, wet your finger tip and gently smooth the point down.

4. Using dry fingers, carefully sprinkle a tiny amount of dry cocoa powder over each cap.

5. Bake for approximately 2¾–3 hours, until the meringues feel dry and crispy to touch, but are still white or mostly white. Oven temperatures may vary, so check on them occasionally starting at around 2 hours.

6. Turn off the oven and allow the meringues to continue to dry out in the closed oven for another hour, or up to overnight. When they have thoroughly cooled and dried, melt the chocolate chips with the coconut oil. This is easy to do using a microwave; heat them for about 30 seconds at a time, stirring in between, until the partially melted chips can be stirred smooth. (Overheating the chocolate may cause it to seize up, or become stiff and difficult to use.)

7. Spread some melted chocolate on the base of each mushroom cap and place the flat end of a stem in the center of the base. Gently place the mushrooms on a parchment paper–lined tray to cool and harden the chocolate. Store at room temperature in an air-tight container; they will store quite well in a fairly cool environment.

Fairies' Bird Nests

MAKES 8 NESTS.

Fairies carefully collect eggs from a variety of birds for their baking and cooking needs, always leaving some in each nest to hatch. They place them in specially woven fairy nests for safekeeping, until they are ready to use them. These tasty little nests remind us of the pretty, sparkly nests fairies are so fond of creating. You will be forming your eggs from white modeling chocolate, which is simply white chocolate that has been melted and quickly combined with a little light corn syrup. It can then be divided and colored as you wish. I like light sky blue and pale ferny green because they are favorite fairy colors. Because the fairies only harvest one egg at a time from any birds' nests they may find, there is always a variety of them in their fairy baskets. That's also why you will notice the eggs in the fairy baskets have different colors. Hint: If you're running short on time, pastel coated Jordan almonds can be substituted for White Chocolate Almond Eggs.

Bird Nests
1 cup white baking chips
¼ cup almond butter
2½ cups crispy chow mein noodles
Sparkling fairy dust

White Chocolate Almond Eggs
4-ounce bar white baking chocolate
2 tablespoons light corn syrup
Food coloring as desired
16 roasted salted whole almonds

1. Melt the white chips with the almond butter by microwaving on high in a microwave-safe bowl for about 30 seconds at a time, until the chips are mostly melted; stir to complete the process. Alternately, place them in a glass or metal bowl and place the bowl over a pan of simmering water, stirring occasionally until they are just melted, again stirring to blend the chips and almond butter smoothly.

2. Using a large spoon or spatula, fold in the crispy chow mein noodles. Form this mixture into 8 even mounds on a waxed paper or parchment-lined baking sheet. Gently form a little depression in the center of each.

3. Sprinkle each nest generously with your preferred fairy dust (I like to use a pretty mixture available through an online company called Fancy Sprinkles, or you can combine a variety of sprinkles and sugars available in most grocery stores). Chill the nests until the chocolate-almond butter mixture is firm.

4. To construct the eggs, break or chop the bar of white chocolate into small pieces; this helps it melt more smoothly. Microwave or melt in a bowl over simmering water until the chocolate is just melted.

continued on next page

5. Next, stir in the corn syrup and desired coloring; this will change the consistency of the melted chocolate into white modeling chocolate. Seal the cooled mixture in a plastic bag or small bowl with tight fitting lid and keep in the refrigerator when not using. It will be softer when at room temperature and harden up when it has been refrigerated. Simply work it around with your warm hands to make it more malleable and easier to form into eggs, or whatever other shapes you may wish.

6. Pinch off about 1 tablespoon of the modeling chocolate for each bird's egg. Wrap it around an almond, covering the entire nut and molding one end slightly smaller than the other. Voilà! You've just created a white chocolate almond egg. Continue until you have 16 eggs in all. Better put them in the nests quickly, before somebody tries to eat them!

CREAMY CHOCOLATE RAINBOW CONES

MAKES 6 CONES.

Ice cream just happens to be another favorite fairy food. Creamy Chocolate Rainbow Cones combine cool, creamy ice cream with the fairies' beloved rainbow colors and fruity flavors. They've even added a bit of chocolate and peanut butter! The rainbow cones are easy-peasy to prepare; once they are filled, simply store in the freezer until you are ready to eat them. If kept properly frozen, the cones and cereal will stay nice and crispy for several days. Creamy Chocolate Rainbow Cones are a fun summertime treat, although they are really quite tasty any time of the year.

6 assorted (rainbow if possible) ice cream
    cones (cup type)
1¼ cups milk chocolate chips
2 tablespoons coconut oil
2 tablespoons peanut butter; crunchy is
    especially nice
1 cup fruit-flavored crispy rice cereal
1 pint of your preferred ice cream

1. Prepare a small baking tin (one large enough to hold 6 cones, but small enough to fit in the freezer) by lining it with baking parchment paper or waxed paper.

2. Melt together the milk chocolate chips, coconut oil, and peanut butter. This is easy to do in a microwave-safe bowl, heating for 30–45 seconds at a time in the microwave. Stir well after each heating segment, until the chips and peanut butter have melted nicely; don't overheat or the chocolate could become thick and hard to work with.

3. Place ¼ cup of the melted chocolate mixture into a smaller bowl; place ½ cup of the fruity cereal on a flat plate. Dip and twirl the top of each cone in the melted chocolate, coating up a bit around the rim. Dip in the cereal to coat well; place, dipped side down, on the parchment lined baking tin.

4. Freeze for 2–3 minutes to firm up the chocolate. Meanwhile, scrape any unused dipping chocolate (there probably won't be much, if any) back into the pan with the rest of the still melted mixture. Using a small spoon, place about a teaspoon of the melted chocolate into the base of each of the six chilled cones, smoothing it around. Add a small amount of the remaining cereal.

5. Now scoop some slightly softened ice cream into each cone, pressing it gently so that it's just about even with the top of each cone. Gently and quickly spread the remaining chocolate over the entire surface of each scoop of ice cream.

6. Sprinkle with the remaining cereal and carefully place upright on the baking tin. The cones may either be eaten while still soft and creamy, or frozen solid, which will take about 4 hours. If they are to remain in the freezer for more than a couple of days, wrap each cone in plastic wrap to help keep them fresh.

Fairies' Amazing Dessert Bowls

MAKES 4 BOWLS.

Fairies' Amazing Dessert Bowls are just perfect for holding ice cream on a hot summer day. Once you have finished eating your ice cream, you can munch and crunch on the bowl itself! Even though a sprinkling of Fruited Fairy Dust makes them almost too pretty to eat, please don't hesitate! They are a delicious way to end your day. As an alternative to ice cream, you might also like to fill your bowls with Strawberry Fairy Fluff (page 91).

4 small latex balloons, inflated to
    approximately 6-inch diameter
Non-stick cooking spray
1½ cups white vanilla candy melts or
    baking chips
Fruited Fairy Dust (page 117) in a variety
    of colors & flavors

1. Prepare the balloons by inflating them just enough to form a bowl the size you'd like it. Tie them tightly shut and gently wash the rounded end of each balloon so that you have a clean surface for dipping. Pat the balloons dry and spray the rounded end of each with non-stick cooking spray; set them aside.

2. Heat the candy melts in the microwave or in a dish over simmering water according to the package instructions, or microwave for 30-second intervals until mostly melted, stirring until it's nice and smooth.

3. Swirl four small, circular bases of melted candy on a parchment-lined baking sheet.

4. Holding each balloon firmly, dip and swirl the clean, rounded end around in the dish of candy melts. Using a slight up and down motion will produce scalloped edges on the bowl-to-be. Make sure you have coated the balloon with a thick covering, especially on the scallops; if it's too thin, the edges may crack when you try to remove the balloon.

5. Quickly place each dipped balloon upright, centering each balloon on one of the circular bases. Using your fingers, sprinkle Fruited Fairy Dust decoratively over each candy melt bowl while the confection is still warm.

6. Allow the dipped balloons to cool and totally harden the candy melts. When you are ready to "unmold" your finished creations, pop the balloons! They may cling a bit to the bowls, but if you are careful, you can pull them away. Dispose of the balloons; they have done their task. Your Fairies' Amazing Dessert Bowls are now ready to be filled, or stored carefully in a cool, dry place for another day.

Pixies' Popcorn

MAKES 4-5 CUPS OF POPCORN.

Popcorn is a favorite fairy snack; they love it hot, sprinkled with salt and drizzled with melted butter, or coated with crunchy caramel or mellow cheese. And they become particularly excited when the pixies bring out this festive, fruity popcorn! It can be made in all sorts of colors and flavors, and there is something sweet, salty, fruity, and crunchy in every bite. Fruit-flavored dry gelatin powder is the secret ingredient that makes Pixies' Popcorn such a unique treat. Because the fruit glaze cooks to an extremely hot temperature, it's important to have adult supervision when making this recipe.

2 tablespoons coconut oil, divided
¼ cup popping corn
½ cup sugar
⅛ teaspoon salt
2 tablespoons light corn syrup
1 tablespoon water
1 tablespoon dry fruit-flavored gelatin
   powder (sugar sweetened)

1. Preheat the oven to 250°. Place a sheet of parchment paper on a large baking sheet and spray lightly with non-stick cooking oil. Lightly oil or spray a large, heat resistant bowl.

2. Pop the popcorn in 1 tablespoon of the coconut oil. This can be done by melting the oil in a two-quart, lidded saucepan over medium high heat. Add the popcorn kernels (they will probably start to sizzle) to the hot pan, cover it with the lid, and allow the corn to pop, occasionally shaking the pan or moving it around on the burner, until the popping has stopped. Remove from heat and open the lid away from you so that the hot steam doesn't burn you. Carefully pour the hot popcorn into the bowl. This should make about 4–5 cups of plain popcorn.

3. In a small saucepan, combine the remaining 1 tablespoon of coconut oil, the sugar, salt, light corn syrup, and water. Bring to a boil over medium heat, stirring constantly. Continue to boil for 1 full minute. Remove from the heat and carefully (it is extremely hot!) stir in the dry gelatin powder. Using a long-handled spoon is the safest way to do this; the mixture will foam up and may splatter a little.

4. Immediately pour the hot syrup evenly over the popcorn in the bowl. Stir it carefully with the long-handled spoon and then pour it evenly onto the prepared baking sheet. Remember to *never* use your fingers or hands to do this; the sugar mixture is extremely hot and will also stick to your skin, which could burn you badly.

5. Place the baking sheet in the oven and bake for approximately 1 hour, stirring gently every 15 minutes. At this point the glaze will have begun to melt a bit again, but not have turned brown. Allow the pan to cool completely before removing the Pixies' Popcorn, breaking it apart if necessary.

6. Store it in airtight containers or zip-lock bags to keep it fresh and crispy. *Hint:* You can also reheat the popcorn in a 250° oven for about 10–15 minutes to restore its crispy texture.

About the Author

The first time Marie remembers seeing fairies, she was about five years old. Her mother showed her the fairy lights shining in the woods on the south side of their meadow. Since Marie was lucky enough to sleep out on her family's back porch during the summer, she was able to observe their little twinkling lights from the comfort of her bright red folding cot. She's not sure if her older brothers enjoyed viewing the fairies as much as she did, but for her, it was the beginning of a life-long friendship.

Marie still lives in the country with her husband and three cats. There is a little fairy meadow behind her house, although sadly she no longer has a back porch or a bright red folding cot. She still loves watching the fairy lights begin to twinkle during the dusky hours of long summer evenings. And now, she has grandchildren to share fairy adventures with, which is even better!

She suspects that the cats occasionally see fairies, too. Fortunately, they have all remained on good terms with one another.

When Marie is not busy hunting for fairies, she loves to cook and create new recipes. Although she has written a few other cookbooks, *Fairy Food* is her favorite! She hopes you will enjoy using it as much as she has enjoyed writing it.

INDEX

CONVERSION CHARTS

METRIC AND IMPERIAL CONVERSIONS

(These conversions are rounded for convenience)

Ingredient	Cups/Tablespoons/Teaspoons	Ounces	Grams/Milliliters
Butter	1 cup/16 tablespoons/2 sticks	8 ounces	230 grams
Cheese, shredded	1 cup	4 ounces	110 grams
Cream cheese	1 tablespoon	0.5 ounce	14.5 grams
Cornstarch	1 tablespoon	0.3 ounce	8 grams
Flour, all-purpose	1 cup/1 tablespoon	4.5 ounces/0.3 ounce	125 grams/8 grams
Flour, whole wheat	1 cup	4 ounces	120 grams
Fruit, dried	1 cup	4 ounces	120 grams
Fruits or veggies, chopped	1 cup	5 to 7 ounces	145 to 200 grams
Fruits or veggies, puréed	1 cup	8.5 ounces	245 grams
Honey, maple syrup, or corn syrup	1 tablespoon	0.75 ounce	20 grams
Liquids: cream, milk, water, or juice	1 cup	8 fluid ounces	240 milliliters
Oats	1 cup	5.5 ounces	150 grams
Salt	1 teaspoon	0.2 ounces	6 grams
Spices: cinnamon, cloves, ginger, or nutmeg (ground)	1 teaspoon	0.2 ounce	5 milliliters
Sugar, brown, firmly packed	1 cup	7 ounces	200 grams
Sugar, white	1 cup/1 tablespoon	7 ounces/0.5 ounce	200 grams/12.5 grams
Vanilla extract	1 teaspoon	0.2 ounce	4 grams

OVEN TEMPERATURES

Fahrenheit	Celsius	Gas Mark
225°	110°	¼
250°	120°	½
275°	140°	1
300°	150°	2
325°	160°	3
350°	180°	4
375°	190°	5
400°	200°	6
425°	220°	7
450°	230°	8

Also Available from Skyhorse

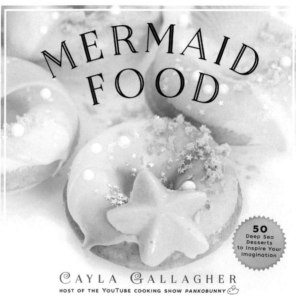